Reach Your Mountaintop

10 Keys to Finding the Hidden
Opportunity in Your Setbacks, Flipping
What You've Heard on Its Head, and
Achieving Legendary Goals

by Jeff Davis

Published by eBookIt.com

Edited by Kelly Huckaby

ISBN-13: 978-1-4566-2755-3

This book is dedicated to the experts featured in this book.
Thank you for all you do.
Because of you, this world is a better place.

What People Are Saying

"From rising out of the pits of an unexpected setback to speaking all over the world, Jeff is helping others reach peaks which previously seemed insurmountable. This book contains the skills, mindset, and tools necessary to take you from where you are to be where you want to be. It's full of wisdom most people don't acquire until late in their lives."

– David Szymanski, entrepreneur

"Absolutely amazing insights, very powerful. This will help people who are struggling and also anyone looking to take their life to the next level. This is filled with hard-hitting content and advice. Jeff has my full endorsement and support."

– Chris Salem, entrepreneur, authentic leadership expert, and professional speaker, christophersalem.com

"*Reach Your Mountaintop* is a must-read for anyone going through a challenge or looking to achieve more. Jeff Davis does a great job of combining research from experts and personal stories to give you a multitude of strategies you can use to make a difference in your attitude and your life."

– Heather Hansen O'Neill, award-winning speaker, author, and founder of L-FOCUS, helping students and business people make a difference in the world, heatherhansenoneill.com

"What I love so much about Jeff's story is that the lessons from it can relate to anyone. You can insert your own story into the moral of Jeff's message and remember that your self-worth does not depend on the outcome of any situation. I recommend this book to anyone who is looking to find the silver lining and take their life to the next level."

– Marc Williams, author, professional speaker, philanthropist, and high school principal, marcwilliamsspeaks.com

"A compelling book...loved the stories, thorough research, and featured experts. A must read for anyone looking to define their own version of success and then follow through with practical steps leading them to their own Mountaintop."

– Mark Strong, coach, trainer, speaker, markstrongcoaching.com

"This book is loaded with great ideas to help you be a better leader and get the most out of yourself."

– Brian Tracy, speaker, entrepreneur, success expert, author of *How the Best Leaders Lead*

"This book does a great job of taking high-level leadership concepts and making them practical. You can apply these tips in your day-to-day life. I also love how Jeff weaves his own thoughts in with the featured experts. If you're ready to move beyond your obstacles and achieve success, read this book."

– Dan Blanchard, author of *The Storm* and a two-time junior Olympian wrestler

"*Reach Your Mountaintop* takes you on a journey where you meet people, all of whom have lessons that we can use to reach our own pinnacle of success. Along the road the author juxtaposes his own life into the scenarios, telling us what he has learned on his own path to the Mountaintop. Along the way we are given the opportunity to learn many lessons, but the author is careful to point out that we must all find our own way, and there is no one way or the right way. The book flows well, giving us opportunities to learn in a manner that is not overwhelming and lets us know that it is okay to make mistakes and fail. The important thing is to keep going, learn from our failures, and we will eventually find our own true path. A wonderful read that hits upon every facet of living a successful life in a manner that challenges us and at the same time allows us to be gentle with ourselves."

– Harvey Deutschendorf, emotional intelligence expert, internationally published author of *The Other Kind of Smart: Simple Ways to Boost Your Emotional Intelligence for Greater Personal Effectiveness and Success* (published in 4 languages), and speaker. To take the EI Quiz go to theotherkindofsmart.com.

"If you're an entrepreneur looking for golden nuggets of high-value content to make your dreams a reality, then look no further. In *Reach Your Mountaintop*, Jeff has mapped out the necessary actionable steps you'll need to trek your way over the massive rock boulders, under the fallen trees, and through the heavy rainstorms, until you push through the clouds and reach the sunny peak of your Mountaintop. Use these well-researched expert words as your inspirational and motivational trail guide to take ACTION!"

— Rick Woods, professional organizer, speaker, author of *Make Room for Clarity*, thefunctionalorganizer.com

"What I love about this book is that it provides the practical tips needed to advance in the career of your choice. I found this book to be very useful, and it came at a great time for me."

— Rob Rowse, accountant, businessman, and economist

"Having gone to the Mountaintop several times myself over the years, it was such a joy to read Jeff's book! This should be required reading for all teens and college students. As for adults, there are golden nuggets for everyone to be inspired by."

— Suzanne Duret, revenue strategist, revenuerevealed.com

"After reading Jeff's story and the experts he's featured, I see that he lives his message. This book shows you how to get past your obstacles, find hidden opportunities, and help other people the way you were meant to. This process will have you clear on what you want so that you can manage your time effectively and achieve your biggest goals."

– Kevin Kruse, New York Times Bestselling Author of *15 Secrets Successful People Know About Time Management* and keynote speaker, kevinkruse.com

Contents

A Note to You, the Reader

There are some compelling stories and examples in this book. All conversations with the experts featured in this book have been printed accurately, and the dialogue is included with their permission. The story I share in the first chapter is fully transparent, genuine, real, and exactly as the situation occurred. The ten keys noted in the subtitle of the book are covered in chapters two through eleven.

With that said, I am not a licensed psychologist or therapist. While experience is the best teacher in my own life, I'm not in any way whatsoever claiming to have all the answers. While these proven methods and insights have worked well for many other people and could work for you, there is no guarantee they will work well for you unless you follow through on what you learn. Do the work to apply these principles in your life and know real change comes from sustained effort over a period of time. Do what works for you and trust your intuition when it comes to figuring out what to apply in your life and what to discard.

If you are in crisis or a challenge, please contact a licensed psychiatrist or a national hotline. While my time is limited due to prior and ongoing commitments, I genuinely care about you and what you're experiencing in your life. If you are too embarrassed to seek help and have exhausted all other options, you can email me directly at jeff@jeffdspeaks.com or get in touch with me on social media. Please consider first reaching out to someone you know, as they may know you and the situation you are dealing with better. But I want you to know there is someone here for you who truly cares, even when you feel completely and utterly alone.

The following pages took more than two years to write, but more than two decades to learn. To respect your time, I've synthesized each chapter so that you can easily read and apply these lessons in your life. I encourage you to write in a journal and reflect on yourself and your life's purpose as you read the book. I'm sincerely excited that we are taking this journey together.

Acknowledgements

Writing a book is no small feat, and I had the help of many people to make this happen. First, I'd like to thank everyone who let me feature them in this book. It means a lot that we connected one-on-one, and you let me share your life story, advice, and insights – I'm sure your words will help and inspire many. Thank you to Dan Blanchard, Dr. Dorothy Martin-Neville, Daniel Midson-Short, Ravi Wettasinghe, Dananjaya Hettiarachchi, Nick Thacker, Geeta Nadkarni, Randy Gage, Jenn Scalia, Chris Salem, Jenny Drescher, Heather Hansen O'Neill, Bill Corbett, Ann Meacham, Mike Shelah, Michael Benner, Christine Southworth, Dave Wheeler, Michael Lynch, John Lee Dumas, Rick Woods, Chip Janiszewski, Michelle Demers, Brian Olds, John Powers, Pat Helmers, Trevor Smith and Harvey Bailey. These authors, speakers, coaches, philanthropists, marketers, entrepreneurs, and leaders are listed at the end of this book with more information if you'd like to get in touch with any of them.

At one point in the book writing and editing process, I lost momentum. I wasn't about to give up, but I wasn't making any progress either. There are four friends in my life who helped get me back into gear by giving me both the encouragement and motivation to finish what I started. A big thank you to Zach Campbell, Ashir Nelson, Heather Hansen O'Neill, and David Szymanski for taking the time to chat with me and helping to rekindle all of the awesome reasons I have to get this book out there to the world.

A special thank you to my good friend and fellow author Dan Blanchard who helped me work out some of the kinks in this book and clean it up. I'd also like to thank speaker Oscar Romero for taking a thorough look at the manuscript and improving it further. And Kelly Huckaby, my editor, I appreciate your expertise and help throughout this process. You guys are brilliant, keep up the great work.

I am incredibly appreciative to my girlfriend as well as my three siblings Jamie, Emily, and Annemarie for believing in me and letting me bounce ideas off of them. Thank you, Mom and Dad, for being there for me during both the good and bad times. I would not be where I am today if it weren't for your support, kindness, and love.

To all my Toastmasters friends through the years, you know who you are. Thank you for all the encouragement and listening to my many speeches. Likewise to my National Speakers Association friends. You guys are the best. To my dear friend Judith Anne Dellosso, who I met through Toastmasters, I miss you dearly. I know you are smiling from above. And to my late Aunt Meg, I wish you were here to read this book. I know you would be proud.

John Powers, thank you for teaching me to keep things in perspective and be the bigger person during challenging situations. Harvey Bailey, thank you for your lifelong friendship. Chris Salem, thank you for being a valuable friend and resource. Brian Olds, you have done more for me than you will ever know. I will never forget the kindness of all of you.

If I didn't mention your name, please know that I am genuinely and incredibly grateful for your help, friendship, and support.

Introduction

We're In This Together

This book encompasses everything that *no one ever told me* when I was in high school and college, but would have been incredibly helpful if someone had. Because I received little to no help in my younger years, I've made it my lifelong mission to share these lessons with as many people as possible. For the record, I had great and supportive parents, but when you are in a society that is constantly dictating to you how to live your life, it is easy for those few helpful voices to get drowned out.

The power behind these tips is that they apply to you at any point in your life. They are *universal principles,* and we will discuss them in detail because they can help you get through a variety of situations and circumstances.

Eckhart Tolle, in *A New Earth: Awakening to Your Life's Purpose*, says, "Nobody can go through childhood without suffering emotional pain. Even if both your parents were enlightened, you would still find yourself growing up in a largely unconscious world."

I had an extremely difficult adolescence and was the quintessential late bloomer, learning all of this the hard way. But I wouldn't wish that on my worst enemy, and that's why the following pages show you the core lessons needed to overcome obstacles, define your own version of success, and revolutionize your life.

What do I mean by late-bloomer? Academically, I was way ahead of the curve. It wasn't like I was a know-it-all or anything like that, I just studied hard and took school seriously. However, I didn't have my growth spurt until my junior and senior years of high school. While my friends were enjoying time with their girlfriends, I was awkwardly wondering if I'd ever be able to approach girls.

I eventually got past it – I just happened to have that transitional stage later than most. Now I'm known as a half-nerd, half-stud. I still retain some of those nerdy elements from my past, but I'm outgoing and easily approach just about anyone. I share this to show that it's possible to revolutionize your life and get past dark times.

I get that setbacks and disappointments are inevitable. And I get that we are all going to have trials and tribulations, ups and downs. But what I don't get is why no one ever gave me the tools necessary to properly work through those challenges.

This book begins with a heartfelt story about a setback I experienced at the end of my high school years. It's a relatively quick story, but I want to give you a better feel for where I'm coming from. The rest of the book covers tips, insights, lessons, and core content from experts I've featured. These experts are entrepreneurs, business owners, coaches, speakers, authors, consultants, marketers, philanthropists, and top employees I've had direct conversations with. I act as a conduit to deliver their wisdom to you. I'll also add my own input and content throughout the book to clarify certain points and give you my perspective, experience, and knowledge, for your benefit.

After hitting rock bottom in my high school years, I'm now an author, professional speaker, and traveler. But it wasn't easy to get there, and there were many setbacks. As you move forward on your own journey, applying these lessons in your life will get you to your next level. After reading this book, you'll laugh at setbacks that cause most people to tremble. You'll be able to pluck success from the jaws of failure and find the silver lining in nearly any situation. And while you're at it, you'll be happier, more fulfilled, and have better balance in life.

It won't always be easy. And the nature of self-growth involves setbacks, twists and turns, and deviations from what was expected. But if you stick with the journey, you'll discover hidden treasures inside of yourself and others you meet.

We're in this together. It's an honor to accompany you on this journey. I promise that if you stay with the experts and me throughout the rest of this book, you'll be in a better place than when you started reading. In addition, you'll be equipped and ready to handle what life may throw at you. This book is an antidote to the way things are – let's dive into this thought-provoking material together.

What Does Reaching Your Mountaintop Mean?
Before we dive into the content, let's make something perfectly clear: reaching the Mountaintop means reaching YOUR Mountaintop. It's not about what others expect or think of you. It's not even about what close friends or family members want from you. Reaching your Mountaintop is about trusting your intuition and moving forward despite what others may say.

Your Mountaintop is usually not a destination or place. It's the feeling or state of mind you get when you stay focused, avoid distractions, and push past roadblocks. The Mountaintop is a way of thinking, acting, and being. It's being more concerned with making an impact and helping those in need than needlessly worrying about the opinions of others.

Being at or near the Mountaintop in each moment means being quintessentially yourself. Just because you haven't met someone else's definition of success does not mean that you haven't reached your Mountaintop. Part of being your best in each moment means releasing the opinions of others and staying true to yourself.

I went from one end of the spectrum (doubting myself nearly every hour of every day) to the other end of the spectrum (being self-assured even during difficult and challenging circumstances). Of course there are always going to be ups and downs, progress and setbacks, but on the whole, it is possible to live each day with confidence, truth, and integrity.

To be clear, this is not some cop-out to suddenly set your goals low so you easily reach them. The goal is to become conscious and clear enough on your own purpose that you refuse to allow anyone else on this planet to dictate your life's path. We all have to sacrifice, we all have to pay the bills, and I *fully* understand what it's like to struggle on a daily basis. But you don't have to settle. This book shows you how you can transcend your limitations in a very real and practical way.

I'm aware that's easier said than done, but it's where we all have to start. Most people doing well now were once doing poorly. Most of us have not had success handed to us on a silver platter – we have to work our butts off for it. But, ironically, it's the climb and hard work that gives us the perspective we need to become the person who attracts success.

I'm humbled to have you on this journey with me, and I will give you the content you need to take your life to the next level. Read the book in its entirety and get a good feel for the overall message. Then pick one or two specific tactics to apply in your life. Don't overwhelm yourself and don't try to change everything at once. Start small. Small, daily changes lead to massive long-term results.

You can act *in spite of* your doubts and use your obstacles as stepping stones. Doubt is not a bad thing as long as we use it as a signpost to continue facing our insecurities and moving forward. We can transmute our doubts, worries, and fears into a positive upward cycle of growth. This book will show you how.

Chapter 1: Why Did No One Tell Me?

"Dear Warden, You were right. Salvation lay within."
– Andy Dufresne, The Shawshank Redemption

Taking Baseball Very Seriously

At seventeen-years-old, baseball was my life. I played on the top summer Connecticut baseball teams, constantly practiced and trained, and dreamed of being a starter for the high school varsity team. Junior year I was on varsity but didn't get any playing time, so I was putting all my hopes and dreams into being a starter spring of my senior year.

When I went to college showcases, I was one of the standout players, and I received seven letters in the mail from interested colleges who wanted me to play for them. I had scouts coming up to me saying, "Wow, you are an incredible hitter and ballplayer."

This was my lifelong dream – a dream I had earned – and nothing was going to stop me. It was my dream since I was three years old.

After all, I was a *college recruit athlete.* I was asked by numerous schools to play at the collegiate level based on scouts witnessing my outstanding performances in showcases, and I committed to a school in Maryland called McDaniel College. I was destined to play college ball in the well-known and competitive Centennial Conference.

In one showcase I went to in New Jersey, competing against the top high school ballplayers from the east coast, I was on fire. I crushed double after double. I did so well that I received many letters in the mail from interested colleges.

Senior year, I performed extremely well in tryouts. As a college recruit athlete, I was, of course, confident, but I was *definitely* not one of those players to be cocky, arrogant, or mean. I was humble, gracious, grounded, and kind (in fact, I was probably TOO nice; after decades of letting people walk all over me, I reinvented myself and learned how to be assertive and stand up for myself – but that's a topic for a different book).

In live scrimmages against other teams, I was one of the only players on our team to consistently hit well. As a soon-to-be college athlete, I was one of the best players in the league.

Why was I so intensely committed to being the best I could be on the field and becoming a starter? Because everyone – I mean EVERYONE – in my high school years told me that my self-worth depended on being on the team. When you hear something often enough, it's hard to ignore it. There's absolutely nothing wrong with trying out for a team, and I love sports. The danger is when you put all of your self-worth into being on that team like I did.

I would frequently hear my classmates saying to myself and others, "You're nothing if you're not an athlete." Over and over and over again – and then over again after that. I'm not blaming my classmates for anything, just stating facts. It was an extremely competitive and dysfunctional atmosphere.

There was a star hockey player at our school who wasn't the most outgoing guy you'd meet, but because he played hockey he was revered. To his credit and defense, he was a genuine guy. One of my so-called friends said, referring to the star, "Without hockey, he'd be nothing." I see now that's a ridiculous statement – the truth is each individual has infinite worth, whether or not they play sports – but at the time I took my friend's statement to heart. I thought to myself, *in order to be worth something, I absolutely must be a starter on the high school baseball team.*

I had another friend who was a big wrestler who said to me, "I'd be nothing without wrestling." The idea that you are nobody without playing a sport was being deeply ingrained into my psyche – my classmates were as misinformed as I was. A common theme at my high school was that if you played a sport, you were somebody, and if you didn't play a sport, you were nobody.

I was letting other people's definition of "success" become my reality, even if their definition was idiotic. I listened to my friends and teachers when they said that in order to be somebody, you have to play a sport (at the time I didn't realize that their definition of success was completely wrong and had no grounding in reality, but because I trusted these people I listened to everything they said).

A Timely Hit

Ready to make my dreams become a reality, I was fully prepared when tryouts rolled around spring of my senior year. I did really well, and my teammates said to me, "Wow, Jeff, you've gone from good to great as a ballplayer and really earned this starting role."

In the final scrimmage of the tryout period against another varsity high school team, I was the starting left fielder. The coaches weren't putting in the scrubs – they were putting in the supposed starters for the season. Although this was a "scrimmage," I assure you it was every bit as real as a game that counts – umpires, cheering fans, and everything else that comes along with a serious baseball game.

The opposing pitcher was a *Division I college recruit* athlete. Division I, my friend – top of the line, the best of the best – one of the greatest pitchers in the world at my age level and that's no exaggeration. He was throwing gas! If you're not already familiar, "throwing gas" is a popular expression in baseball for pitchers who throw extremely hard and fast and are very difficult to hit.

He struck out some of our best hitters, including our captain! Very few of our players could get a hit off of him and when they did they were weak infield singles. He had walked a few guys, but no one on our team even came close to scoring. In my first at-bat against him, batting 7th in the lineup, I hit a hard groundball to second base, but right at the second baseman. I was out at first.

But I knew I could get a hit off of this guy. All of those many summer baseball games, competing against the absolute best baseball players in the United States of America – playing in tournaments in Florida, Pennsylvania, Ohio, New York, and Connecticut, and being considered by teammates and opposing coaches as one of the best players on the field – were paying off.

I got up again with two men out. I took a couple of low pitches and went up on the count 2-0. I then fouled a pitch off and took a close-call strike 2. The count was now 2-2. I stared down the formidable pitcher. *This was it. This was my moment.*

It was now or never. Even though I was a good player, I seemed to get this constant judgmental vibe from the coach. I was as friendly as possible to him and worked my butt off every step of the way, but nothing seemed to work.

I knew I had to be a definite and guarantee for the starting left fielder spot because of my track record, abilities, and work ethic, but I took this at-bat very seriously because it was a chance to prove myself once and for all to the coach.

The pitch was his best fastball, about chest-high. With my mind still and my focus at an all-time high, I turned on his pitch and had one of the best hits of my entire life. It was a double off of the fence, almost a home run. When I got to second base, even the shortstop of the opposing team looked at me and said, "Nice hit, man."

My teammates were celebrating in the dugout, yelling out all sorts of supportive comments. The fans were clapping and cheering for me. I felt like a million bucks.

I made it. I did it. I finally proved myself. I am finally somebody.

We were getting crushed and down by nine runs, but the reason why everyone was so happy was because someone finally got a good hit off of this incredibly foreboding and highly skilled opposing pitcher.

Unexpected News in the Locker Room

On the bus ride back to the locker room after this final day of scrimmaging against another team, I was on cloud nine. I had a good game and proved myself. *Years* of hard work and sacrifice were finally coming to fruition. One of my best friends and the captain of the team said to me, "Everyone is talking about you being our starting left fielder Jeff. You've really earned this."

When we got back to the locker room, we all sat down on the bench. The head coach took out the list of names of people who made the team and read the names.

My name wasn't called at first. I figured my name must be towards the bottom of the list...but he got to the bottom of the list, and my name *still* wasn't called.

I was cut from the team.

College recruit athlete, one of the best players on the team, and an expected starter by most of my teammates... but I was flat-out cut from the team. I know that doesn't make any sense, but it's a statement of fact that many college scouts told me I'm an outstanding player. I say this to remind you that other credible people are the ones who told me that I'm a fantastic player. But when it came to my high school I simply wasn't one of the coach's favorites (to this day I don't know why) and it was what it was.

It was the worst, most devastating feeling of my life. It's a feeling I can't properly describe in words through this page. It's a feeling I wouldn't wish on anyone.

After I got cut I went in and talked to the head coach along with his assistant; they gave me some generic cop-out answers, but no specific reasons or explanation as to why I didn't make the team. For some reason, they were mostly silent. I was stunned and broken.

I was beyond devastated – I was destroyed. On the drive home, all I could think was, *I'm nobody, I'm nothing, and I'm worthless.* Those horrible thoughts kept playing in my head like a broken record.

I'm nobody, I'm nothing, and I'm worthless. My life is over. It is truly and forever over. I'll never get past this for as long as I live.

At one point I had to pull over. I clenched at my chest, not being able to process or comprehend reality. I've never felt so terrible in my entire life. I had *100%* of my self-worth caught up with being on this team...every last bit of my self-worth.

The Dark Night of My Soul

When I got home, my parents were loving and supportive, but I pushed them away because I was so upset. They tried to help, but I insisted they leave me alone. I isolated myself, terrifying thoughts running through my mind: *I'm nothing. My life is over. I will never be able to show my face to the world again. All my years of hard work are wasted.*

I called my best friend (the captain) up on the phone, and he said, "You know, Jeff, I just have to tell you – no one really cares that you didn't make the team." Was this the same guy who was telling me on the bus all those positive things about me becoming a starter?

Maybe he was being a good friend. After all, he did try to make me feel better in a male macho way. With that said, being a macho male is not always the best way to be. Let's put down our tendencies to be tough in front of people and start showing a softer, kinder, more vulnerable side. For more on this, watch Joe Ehrmann's TEDx talk "Be a Man" on YouTube. I was in the audience when he did this in Baltimore in 2013. As Joe powerfully discussed, being a man is not what you think it is.

With all my self-worth flushed down the toilet, my dreams gone, and embarrassed to the full extent possible, I was wondering why I was born. I was ready to end my life. For as long as I could remember, my life purpose was to be a star baseball player. Now that it was taken from me for reasons beyond my control, I was at a loss and questioning everything. I felt like there was no reason for me to continue living.

Have you ever been so zoomed-in on something that you completely lost yourself in it? That was exactly what I was experiencing and because it was ripped from me so unexpectedly, I truly no longer wanted to be alive.

Senior year turned out to be the worst year of my life after everyone told me that it would be the best year of my life. The happy endings we see in movies don't always exist in reality, and nothing is what it seems. At the time, my life had become a nightmare from which I couldn't escape.

I went to the garage, grabbed the rope from the workbench, and considered hanging myself from the tree out back. I needed to get out of the enormous psychological pain I was in, and I thought this was the solution.

With the rope in my hands, I looked up at the tree.

But just before taking my own life, one last spark of hope came to me that said, "Put the rope down, go up to your room, and go to sleep. You will get through this. Someday you will be able to use this experience to help other people."

Thankfully, I listened to my intuitive voice from within the center of my heart, soul, and psyche. *I listened to that spark, a message from the infinite mind, which came to me through my heart and the very core of my being. You have a spark in your core that will get you through your most difficult moments.*

Back to My Room

I went back up to my room very slowly. I couldn't process or comprehend reality anymore, and nothing seemed to matter. I had to take life one breath at a time.

I laid down on my rug in my room near my bed.

I'm nothing.

I couldn't shake that thought.

I'm nothing.

All my high school friends and coaches told me for many years that in order to be somebody, I had to be an athlete – including teachers and administrators. When you hear something enough times, it's hard to ignore it, and when you internalize it, it becomes your reality. It was my identity, who I was. Without it, I truly felt like nothing. This was beyond perception being reality. This was years of brainwashing turning against me in the worst way possible. I was so certain that I'd be on the team and *be somebody*, that I never once even considered the possibility of not making the team. When I got cut, I literally didn't know if I could go on with my life.

Meditating, I still felt incredibly depressed, but I somehow was becoming aware of my thoughts and emotions from a slightly more objective point of view. If my life were a movie, I was stepping into the seats of the audience instead of getting caught up in the individual scenes.

Horrible thoughts continued to rage – I definitely still hated myself and no longer wanted to be alive, but the more intense the hatred for myself grew the more aware I became of the hatred itself.

At the rock bottom worst moment of my life, something remarkable happened. I was suddenly filled with a deep, overriding sense of peace.

I realized deep down in my soul that my self-worth did NOT depend on being on the team (despite everything I heard, felt, and believed up until that moment) and that everything would be alright. What caused this realization?

Observing my mind and being the witness to my thought process instead of letting an unexpected setback beyond my control dictate who and what I was.

It was more than just a peaceful feeling. With my eyes closed, I felt as if I were entering into some kind of soothing light. Yes, I was definitely still present within my body (no out-of-body experience or anything like that), but psychologically it was as if an outer force was acting to alleviate my pain and suffering – cradling me and keeping me safe.

I no longer felt like an isolated fragment, separate from everyone else. I *was* the universe itself. I no longer felt controlled by the judgments of others.

I felt infinite – free, happy, and joyous – and it was the first time in months (maybe years) that I was not worried about the burden of having to someday *be somebody*. I was simply in the present moment, bathing in peace and love.

I'm a skeptical person, so I would not have thought something like this would happen, but since I experienced it, my entire paradigm of what's possible in life shifted.

Even though my self-worth was gone and I had no hope at an external level, internally a deep wellspring of joy pervaded my being. At a core level, I sensed that someday I would be able to use this unexpected event as a way to connect with others and help people get through their own moments of rock bottom.

I've gone on to share this story with tens of thousands of people around the world as a youth keynote speaker, and many students have told me this speech changed their life. I say that not to impress you in any way whatsoever, but rather to show that you can use your worst moments as a springboard to help others and make a difference in the world.

We all have things that we care passionately about, sometimes to an unreasonable and unhealthy extent. While our individual situations and circumstances are vastly different, feelings are what connect us and are universal. The feeling of devastating loss is the same.

Do you know what is most amazing about experiencing a moment of feeling like nothing? After that, you have nothing to fear. You know that no matter what happens to you, you can handle it. You can be thrown straight into the wolves and yet you'll come out a better person.

From an objective point of view, I went on to experience setbacks that were worse than not making some stupid baseball team. For example, a former boss of mine embezzled company funds and never paid me my hard-earned money from my success as a salesman. While traveling, I went completely broke (not one penny in my bank account) and had no money to eat. But because I already knew what it was like to feel like nothing from a psychological point of view, struggle and hardship had less power over me. I'm able to stay action-oriented in precarious situations and find solutions. I now laugh in the face of fear and move past devastating setbacks from a higher perspective.

This doesn't mean that I'm immune to bad days or down moments, but it does mean that I will pick myself up if things go wrong. And so can you.

When You Feel Like Your Life is Over

We all have things that we care passionately about, sometimes to an unreasonable and unhealthy extent. But when those things that we care about most dearly are taken from us for reasons beyond our control (to this day I still have no idea why my coach cut me), you don't need to go to the extreme, as I did.

Through discussions with hundreds of people in my travels around the world, extensive research, and my transformation over almost a decade from someone literally on the brink of suicide to a genuinely joyful guy who helps others, I've discovered tips and insights we can all apply to get us through our dark nights of the soul, those moments when we truly feel like our life is over. Here are the tips:

- **Take it one breath at a time – literally.** Put down the million and one things from your past that you are upset about, and the billion and one things in your future you are anxious about, and simplify life down to one moment, *this moment*. Just before I was about to hang myself, I used individual breaths to take me out of my downward spiral of self-hatred. If I could use this technique successfully under such extreme circumstances, chances are that you could successfully use it too for the things that are bothering you.

- **Keep it in perspective.** The tendency of the human mind is to zoom in on situations and make a big deal of them, especially when your heart and soul are involved in the outcome. We live in a huge world with a vast array of possibilities, and even though it doesn't seem like it at the moment, your best days are ahead of you and your life is not ruined. Dan Blanchard, author of *The Storm* and a two-time junior Olympian wrestler, says that your past does not equal your future and that your glory days are still in front of you.

• **Instead of trying to think positively, shift back to neutral**. When you are very depressed – at rock bottom, with no hope like I was – the last thing you want is to be overly positive. Imagine driving your car and instead of putting it into drive, you are slowly shifting from reverse back to neutral; instead of fighting your thoughts, choose to be the observer of your thoughts.

• **Your self-worth is infinite**. Your self-worth does not depend upon external circumstances such as making or not making a team or getting a job or doing a particular activity. Nor does it depend on what others think of you.

• **You are loved**. I know it may not feel like it, and I absolutely understand the feeling of embarrassment that you'll never be able to talk about what you are going through, but even when you feel most isolated, I promise there are people who still love you dearly. Don't isolate yourself during tough times.

• **Remember that there is a hidden opportunity in every setback**. When one door closes, another one opens. You can use setbacks to your advantage, and a crisis is an opportunity for a breakthrough. Joel Osteen always says that setbacks are setups for comebacks.

- **This unexpected and unfair situation you are going through (or have already been through) is the *very* situation life wants you to experience to get you to your next level.** At the age of seventeen, with my biggest dream of being a starter on the high school varsity baseball team shattered to pieces, I never would have thought life could get better after such a setback, but it did.

The truth is you can handle any challenge life hands you. The temporary feeling of rock bottom will go away when you realize just how connected and important you are. You have a purpose, and you will help others.

Why Did No One Tell Me?

I'll never understand, for as long as I live, why NOT ONE person told me that my self-worth doesn't depend on being on some silly team. The people I went to high school with were as brainwashed as I was when it comes to what really matters in life.

But you know what? I can't control those people I went to high school with and I peacefully wish them well, as they were also under the spell of this kind of thinking. However, what I can control, in this present moment, are the experiences and lessons I share with the world. And I'm here to tell you that there is *always* a solution and a way out, even when you think all possible options and solutions have been exhausted. It may take some time to figure out, but there is a way forward, even if it means utilizing a backup plan.

Just remember that no matter how badly you feel right now, you will get through your predicament and end up using it to your advantage in a positive way. You will find the silver lining and do incredible things with your life.

What Can We Learn From This?

In the grand scheme of things, making or not making a high school team is not a big deal. Even though I was a college recruit athlete, I didn't have to go into the depths of despair after not making the team. *But no one ever told me that making or not making the team is not a factor in my self-worth. That's why I'm so passionate about spreading this message with others.*

This lesson applies to many other parts of life. Your self-worth doesn't depend on getting or not getting a job. Your self-worth doesn't depend on a relationship working out or not working out. Your self-worth doesn't depend on any of the other myriads of external influences you deal with on a daily basis. Always do your absolute best, but don't attach your self-worth to the result.

Did you know that one in ten people consider suicide? Everybody wants someone who cares and understands them but is often deprived of that. I understand how ridiculously hectic life can get, but if we are too busy to take a minute to share important lessons with our kids, friends, classmates, family, coworkers, colleagues, and acquaintances, then we are missing the boat of what matters most.

Knowing that your self-worth doesn't depend on the outcome of the goal you are striving for is the first big lesson of this book. It's the core of what no one ever told me in high school and college. It's the opposite of what society tells us on a daily basis. Here it is:

Your self-worth does not depend on external circumstances.

This lesson will liberate you and help you to go after what you want with full force, while also allowing you to detach from the outcome (detachment is something Deepak Chopra talks about in *The Seven Spiritual Laws of Success*). You were made to dream big dreams and go after them, but you were *not* made to attach your self-worth to the result. Whenever you are dealing with someone's negative opinion, an unfair circumstance, or other kinds of unexpected events, remind yourself daily that your self-worth doesn't depend on any external factors or results. The irony here is that when you stop getting so caught up in the outcome and instead focus on what's in your control, you'll attract true success.

Using this core realization as your starting point will allow you to really run with all of the lessons in the rest of the book as you move from where you are to where you want to be.

Case Study: Newtown High School

Before we leave this chapter, I'd like to share with you a case study of a school that does an excellent job of running their athletic programs and administration. This is important for two main reasons. First, it's very important to focus on what's right and what can be done moving forward. Second, this is not a book of theory; it's a book of practical, real-world advice you can apply in your life. This case study is a great example of a school actually applying the changes we discussed in this chapter.

Newtown is the town I grew up in and although I didn't go to Newtown High School – I went to a private high school in Fairfield, CT, instead – I'm very well-connected in Newtown, having went to Sandy Hook Elementary School, Newtown Middle School, and frequently taking part in the town's activities. I went to Newtown High School to chat with Dr. Lorrie Rodrigue, the principal, to discuss some of these topics and principles.

"Do you think coaches could do a better job of helping their players keep the game in perspective and not get so caught up in it?" I asked Dr. Rodrigue.

"We do support and guide coaches to support the other side of sports, like teamwork, cooperation, and things like that," replied Dr. Rodrigue. "We also help students to feel good about themselves; we want them to look back on their high school sports experience and feel good about it. It's normal to be competitive, and we can't force it to not be that way, but we can let students know that sports are an opportunity for them beyond just winning and losing a game."

"That's excellent," I said. "I wish someone would have sat me down and told me that when I was in high school. It took you less than a minute to tell me that, but no one sat me down and told me that sports are more than just wins and losses, making the team or not making the team. I was told over and over again that my self-worth 100% depended on being on the team and doing well."

"Who told you that?" Dr. Rodrigue asked me.

"Many of my classmates told me that," I said. "Friends told me that. But it was beyond just my peers, as they were normal kids and I wouldn't have expected them to know all the answers. It was also teachers and administrators who told me that. That's where the situation became dysfunctional – I looked up to these people and took their word for what they were saying. It wasn't a pleasant experience.

"I was a college recruit athlete and when I got cut from the high school team my senior year I was devastated."

"Yes, I definitely get why you were feeling down about that," Dr. Rodrigue said. "Remember that coaches are human too. Sometimes they make the wrong decision. Sometimes they cut the wrong person and end up regretting it. Coaches make mistakes."

"Players need to make sure their self-worth isn't caught up in the outcome," I said. "Make the team or get cut, win the game or lose the game, your self-worth does not depend on that. That's what no one told me in my high school years."

"It is important players know not to tie their self-worth to the outcome of the tryout or game," Dr. Rodrigue said. "And you did touch on part of society's problem here. It's about playing the game for fun. It's about going out for a sport and knowing your life isn't over if you don't make it. You're not always going to be on top, and knowing that lesson will serve someone for the rest of their life. We need to make sure our kids have grit: they need to have the attitude if they don't get it this time, they could get it next time."

"That's awesome, very well said," I replied. "And that's what Newtown High School does well. Are there other factors that go into this philosophy as well?"

"Yes," Dr. Rodrigue said. "It's very easy for a player to let their self-worth get wrapped up in it all. There are financial and all sorts of variables here that can leave kids devastated. There can also be pressure. That's where parenting comes in. When my son was playing basketball, sometimes he would take it very seriously and be incredibly upset and devastated if things didn't turn out the way he wanted them to. I would help him through that and explain it's not life or death. It takes a village to raise a child, so each player has other influences in their lives that can help them deal with challenges."

"Yes, that makes sense," I said. "I have two great parents. At the same time, I was around so many people in my high school who took sports as life and death that I became that way myself. It is true that you become who you surround yourself with. That's why I'm so careful nowadays to surround myself with winners."

Sports do matter and are a positive part of students' lives. At the same time, athletes don't have to let their self-worth get caught up in the outcome.

"It's definitely important to remind the kids that *it's a game*. There's a health factor here too," Dr. Rodrigue said. "If kids are basing their entire lives on one sport, that's unhealthy. But if they can be taught to think of sports like every other extracurricular, they'll benefit from participating in it. Sports are more positive than negative."

"This is great," I said. "Love what you're saying here. Once players are given the right framework to participate in them, I can see how it can be very positive. I made friends on the teams I played on, which was one positive aspect outside of the sport itself."

"Yes," Dr. Rodrigue said. "Whether it's a teacher, coach, parent, college scout, friend, or anyone else, we must ensure the message is this: win or lose, make the team or not make the team, let's have fun. Whatever you do, give it your best, but let's have fun. There are positive experiences in everything – it's all about how you handle setbacks. If players can learn how to handle things that didn't go perfectly well, even unexpected things, then they will be developing grit, which is a crucial quality for success in life."

This concept of self-worth doesn't just apply to sports – it applies to everything you are doing in your life. Go after your goals with full preparation, effort, and to the best of your abilities. But always have fun and remember that it's just something you are doing and *not who you are*. Get rid of labels and participate in life's activities with a detached ease.

Onward and Upward

Let's now hear from other experts as we move into the rest of the book, learning about more lessons people don't talk about nearly enough. *Our society tends to not talk about the things that matter most.* This book is changing that. As you read these lessons, feel free to let me know your thoughts and which lessons or stories resonate with you the most. My email is jeff@jeffdspeaks.com or davisjeffrey222 @gmail.com. I would genuinely love to hear from you.

Ready to create an incredibly powerful mindset and hear from some brilliant, world-renowned experts? Let's do it.

Questions for Reflection

1. What are some ways in which your self-worth is identified with the external world?

2. In what areas or situations in your life have you been giving your power away?
3. How can you become more aware of these people-pleasing tendencies and gently reclaim your inner strength?

Chapter 2: Developing the Mountaintop Mindset

"Three billion people on the face of the earth go to bed hungry every night, but four billion people go to bed every night hungry for a simple word of encouragement and recognition."
– Cavett Robert

As we dive into specific tactics, strategies, and methods you can use to move forward with your life, grow, and evolve, always remember that the Mountaintop is not so much a place as it is a way of being and a state of mind. In harnessing your self-worth and disregarding the opinions of others, know that there are going to be constant ups and downs. But if you implement what we will discuss here you will build a strong foundation to more easily transcend the storms of life.

As you know, no one ever told me that my self-worth didn't depend on an external circumstance such as playing a sport. I always had a choice and my power was buried inside the center of my psyche and soul all along, but I didn't realize this until long after my sports career was over. **Your power is already within you – you just need to uncover it.** This is not some motivational saying; this is a real, practical fact.

Although high school baseball was often a nightmare, I went on to play baseball at the collegiate level. As I mentioned earlier, I was a college recruit athlete, and there were many college scouts out there impressed by my playing abilities. I also went on to play baseball out in Europe, competing against players who played in the minor league (the minor league is the level above college and below the major league). This shows that if you love something to the core, you don't have to let other people stop you from doing it, regardless of what they think. There will be many roadblocks, delays, and setbacks, but ultimately YOU are the only person who can *permanently* stop you. Other people may *temporarily* stop you or momentarily delay you, but you always have the final say in the long-run.

Life may certainly be very unfair at times, but it does have some built-in balancing mechanisms that allow you to find the silver lining and move forward despite undesirable situations.

Stay Humble

In order to fully take control of your life and protect your self-worth from the fake and foolish actions of others, you must develop the Mountaintop mindset of continuously learning, growing, evolving, and pushing forward. This includes remaining humble. Don't give in to your ego. It's a normal human tendency to have an ego, but don't let it overcome you – keep it in check. Have confidence and associate with the right people, but always treat others with respect, even when they're criticizing you. If you become arrogant, you may still make a difference in the lives of others, but you won't be perceived as authentic. Assertiveness is good, but arrogance is bad.

For example, a big-time travel blogger, who I'll respectfully leave nameless, severely criticized me in a phone conversation. Please know I'm all for constructive feedback and I invite people to always be honest with me (and I'm just using this as an example; no hard feelings here). With that said, he came out of nowhere and started to disparage me and put down my first book, *Traveling*

Triumphs: The Improbable in Budapest and Beyond. This guy had a big ego and did not think twice about putting me in my place. While it's great that he has so many followers on social media and I genuinely admire his success, it doesn't give him a right to treat people like garbage.

The weird part about this conversation is that it was my first, and last, conversation with this guy. It's something I can laugh about now, but what I realized from the conversation is that some people let success go to their head. He wasn't humble at all, and he came across as an unkind person. It's absolutely fantastic that he achieved success in the travel blogging world, but his inability to treat newcomers to the industry with respect will limit his ability to climb higher towards the Mountaintop.

Face your doubts head on. Feel your feelings, face them directly, and watch as you are able to laugh at circumstances that terrify many. Look within for your answers regardless of what other people tell you to do. If it matches up with the advice from others, great. But if your inner guidance doesn't agree with the input and suggestions from others, don't let that faze or stop you for one second. One of the biggest regrets of the dying is that they weren't always true to themselves. Don't let that happen to you. Know it's never too late to turn things around. If you're alive and breathing, you still have opportunity to make things better by following your own unique inner voice.

Don't Crash

As with so many other things in life, developing the Mountaintop mindset is a catch-22. You reach your best life and achieve Mountaintop moments by staying grounded and serving others (genuinely, without false pretense). You become successful when you are too busy to wonder whether you are a success or failure because you are so focused on helping others, creating change, and achieving more. The feeling of "Mountaintop" is about being true to yourself, disregarding people who criticize and judge you, and deciding to live out your life's purpose even when the chips are down and the odds are against you.

To be clear – and to take it from someone who has been used by many people with ulterior motives – helping others does not mean, in any way whatsoever, that you let others abuse you, take advantage of you, or cheat you. Stand up for yourself respectfully and say no when necessary. Also, don't ever be afraid to speak up and let others know how you feel. I'm simply suggesting to you to adopt the Mountaintop *mindset* of being kind, serving others, and becoming a bigger person than your naysayers. Take each situation of your life on a case-by-case basis and do what's right for you. Use your Mountaintop mindset as a guiding mechanism to navigate life's inevitable trials and tribulations.

I've found in my experience a great irony: the moment I think I'm doing well and succeeding, life has a way of knocking me back down, putting me in my place, and humbling me. Yet, the moment I think I'm failing and all is lost, life has a way of unexpectedly showing me that my efforts *do* matter, especially when I didn't realize people were taking note of my actions after all. Some examples that show I am making a difference are emails or letters from people looking forward to my next book, when I bump into an old friend who saw one of my YouTube videos and he or she loved the message, or getting feedback that one of my blog posts helped someone make an important decision or overcome a challenge.

One of the challenges of life is that we tend to hear more from our critics than our supporters. Critics tend to be vocal and mean. Know that even if you don't see it or realize it, you are making a difference in the lives of others.

Just like the government, life has its checks and balances, a built-in seesaw system. If you chase after success, it will always seem to elude you, similar to chasing your own shadow and never being able to grasp it. But if you become the person you'd like to attract into your life, filled with character, morals, values, and ethical standards of kindness, success and other people who embody these characteristics will find you.

By all means, maintain a sense of confidence and belief in yourself, but don't let big wins cause you to get a big head about yourself. That's why it is so crucial for it to be *your* Mountaintop. If you get a big head about yourself because other people love you, you'll fall into the gutter when other people hate you – as I did at the end of my high school years. As my good friend Dr. Dorothy Martin-Neville, a successful professional speaker, says, "Always stay down-to-earth. If you get too high on yourself, you will have a crash." Again, I'm all for genuine confidence and self-esteem; just remember to stay even-keeled.

If you reach the top only to find that you climbed the wrong ladder, what's the point? That's not really success, is it? Instead of being addicted to basing yourself on the whims and moods of others, why not stay independent of other opinions and be yourself? True success is about fulfilling your inner life and doing what YOU want, not what others expect of you. Put your ladder against the wall where YOU want to put it, regardless of what it pays.

Money is only one very small measure of success. Just because someone has lots of money doesn't necessarily mean they are successful and fulfilled on the inside. What's important, though, is that they're hopefully making progress on a journey they've chosen, not what someone else chose for them.

Daniel Midson-Short, a fellow speaker and kindred spirit from Australia now living in California, said in one of his powerful speeches, "Letting others dictate your life's path is like giving someone else the remote control to your life. The sense of expectation and obligation to others will always be there, but sometimes the bravest thing you can do is just be you and do what you want to do."

Powerful words – they encapsulate one of the core themes of this book in two sentences! I love how humble and precise Daniel is, and he lives what he teaches. I first met him in Kuala Lumpur, Malaysia, while we were both competing in the semifinals of the World Championship of Public Speaking. He was in a different semifinal grouping that went before mine, and I had the pleasure of watching his speech. It was about the power of putting down our phones and actually paying attention to life. Most of us are addicted to being online and are missing out on our lives. The key here is that when you get to know yourself better and pay attention to the little things, you'll be less inclined to let other people determine your life's direction. Awareness is essential.

As you grow in confidence and implement this Mountaintop mindset, remember that you don't have to follow everyone's advice. This is a deceptively simple tip.

And it's very helpful to keep it in mind when you are around people who want you to conform to their expectations. These people usually mean well and have good hearts. However, they're people with their own opinions, and you have every right to respectfully disregard their input.

The people you look up to are normal human beings. They have flaws and quirks like the rest of us. In my own evolution as a person, what I've found is that everyone is just a person: nothing more, nothing less. Please know that this is not disparaging or putting down anyone as each individual is infinitely worthy of our respect. I simply want us to acknowledge our own power and realize that we have just as many gifts, talents, and potential as anyone else. It's also knowing that we can live life to our own standards, without giving in to the demands and pressures of others.

Remember What Got You Here

Ravi Wettasinghe is from San Diego, California. I became friends with him in the Dominican Republic. We were there with a group of people to help feed and house some of the less fortunate members of the Dominican Republic who chop crops with a machete for a living and barely have enough to survive. Ravi is studying at Quinnipiac University's Medical School, focusing on infectious disease. He is brilliant and an all-around awesome and genuine guy. It was a pleasure to get to know him and become friends with him on this trip.

"It is so incredibly important to embrace the process and focus on the hard work it takes to be successful," Ravi said. "I've found that success, paradoxically, can become a roadblock because when you start getting complacent and stop growing, that's when you'll fall and lose the very success you once had.

"Remember what got you to where you are," Ravi said. "Was it sitting around and doing nothing all the time, or was it staying hungry, focused, and determined to get to the next level?"

Ravi is all for downtime and relaxation too. However, what he's really talking about here is the *exact* thing we've been discussing in this chapter: developing, cultivating, harnessing, and implementing the Mountaintop mindset of being humble, always learning, and not getting a big head. Always treat your learning, growth, and personal development as a never-ending process.

"Success is absolutely fantastic," Ravi said, "but don't ever think you're better than someone else. You may have done different things and chosen to do different activities, but you're not more valuable or worthy than they are as a human being."

Ravi's grounded nature is inspiring, to say the least. Like everyone else I've featured in this book, Ravi's character is top-notch, and he puts into action what he shares here with us. Now let me be very clear: I've gone to great lengths to only feature people in this book who are men and women of their word. And Ravi is one of them.

Celebrate your success. Have some fun. And spend some time with your friends and family. Give yourself a break once in a while. And never forget to continue implementing the hard work ethic that got you to where you are in the first place. Beware, though, if you let your values and ethics go because you are making progress and achieving, you may lose the very success you attained.

To make sure we are on the same page here: it is absolutely alright to realize that you have better character than someone else and that their values don't align with yours. And self-confidence, which comes from knowing and embracing your value, is a valuable quality to have. However, this does not mean you're an intrinsically better or more worthy person than other people, nor does it mean you are judging others. It means that you've become more aware of what you value most. In turn, it is within your right to not be around people who bring you down or who don't reflect where you're going with your life.

"Make sure what you are going after is what YOU want," Ravi said. "If your Mountaintop includes less career and more time spent with family, then make sure to include that in your own equation. Just because someone is doing better than you in one area doesn't mean they are more successful than you. Someone may have reached the pinnacle of their career, but forgotten about friends and family."

As Ravi knows well, there is more to true success than meets the eye. Success is an inside job, and most of it consists in the makeup of your invisible inner world, not your visible outer world. As Jim Rohn said, "Your inner life is reflected in your outer life."

Ravi isn't saying that any one version of success is better or worse than any other version. He's saying that you need to make sure you are finding the right balance and aspects of life that work for *you*. If you want more time with family, then adjust some other area of your life to make it happen.

"If you are burned out from chasing this idea of success, it might be time to stop and learn to enjoy each day," Ravi said. "If your body is telling you to slow down, then listen to what you need. Work extremely hard and never give up, but don't go so over-the-top that all other areas of your life fall to pieces. That's why you must do what works for your specific situation."

Ravi says it best and is the true embodiment of the Mountaintop mindset: it's not about reaching some distant pinnacle and then calling it quits. It's about creating a sustained attitude, habit, and way of living that allows you to embrace challenges and obstacles like a true winner and champion. Win, lose, or tie, your new mindset will allow you to handle the twists and turns of life.

Listen to the Inner Longings

When your self-worth is tied to what other people think, you will sit back and get complacent when everyone approves of you, even if what you've done hasn't satisfied your inner longings. While writing my first book, *Traveling Triumphs: The Improbable in Budapest and Beyond,* three years ago, I was going to graduate school at Johns Hopkins Carey Business School, where I completed a two-year Master's degree program in one year. Additionally, I was working for the Charles County government, which was a two-hour drive one way from Baltimore down into southern Maryland. I was also traveling, growing my speaking business, and constantly doing the networking required to take my initiatives to the next level.

If I had chosen not to write a book, not one person on the planet would have questioned me amidst my intensely busy schedule during those days. But I knew something was missing in my life, and when I listened to my true self,

I realized that I needed to write a book at this point in my life, regardless of how busy I was.

I had an absurdly busy schedule, and I wouldn't be exaggerating to tell you that I had about 15 to 30 minutes of free time a day. But that was enough – I would do my best to dedicate at least 15 minutes a day to the book. Sometimes I only wrote for five to seven minutes or even less. Other days, I could squeeze in an entire lunch break or even a whole hour at the end of the day. And on the weekends, after finishing my homework, I would decline invitations from friends to hangout so that I could write and edit for hours. I know what I did was a sacrifice, but it takes discipline, dedication, and sacrifice in the short-run to get what you want in the long-run. As Jerry Rice said, "Today I will do what others won't, so tomorrow I can accomplish what others can't."

The mindset here is that you must focus on fulfilling your inner life before worrying about outer success. Yes, I obviously wasn't shirking my responsibilities at Johns Hopkins, as it was an incredibly challenging school with concepts I'd never been exposed to before. But when my classes for the day were done, and I was done with work and homework, I decided to do what TRULY gave my life meaning and purpose. By writing and working on my book, I made myself happy. In nearly any situation, at any time, you can do the same.

Always Be Learning

I had the pleasure of meeting Dananjaya Hettiarachchi in Kuala Lumpur, Malaysia, after he won the World Championship of Public Speaking in 2014. I was out there in Kuala Lumpur competing in the same contest, and I lost at the semifinals level. Overall, I had a wonderful experience. Dananjaya is the well-deserved champion and every single person in that 3,000-member audience knows what a terrific speaker he is.

Dananjaya was getting bombarded by people after he won, as expected, but I somehow managed to talk to him. To his credit, he didn't dismiss me or appear stressed at all: he embodied the Mountaintop mindset in its fullest by doing his best and showing the world what he's made of. He remained centered, humble, and grounded.

He lives on the other side of the world in Sri Lanka. I followed up with him after I got back home to the United States, via LinkedIn and other social media, and we have stayed in touch since then.

Dananjaya's wisdom encompasses two central and extremely important points:

- You have to first BE something before you can have that something.
- Always be learning.

Dananjaya was the champion even before he was crowned the official champion because of the way he carried himself, the way he was *being*. I discussed this with fellow Toastmasters friends after the competition was over. Yes, his speech was amazing and brilliant, not to mention flawless and perfectly thought out – but beyond that, it was his demeanor, attitude, and his *way of being* that got him to the top (note: this is something we will return to at the end of this book when we hear from speaker and professional coach Harvey Bailey).

By being the champion, carrying himself like a winner, being kind to others, delivering a speech that helps and serves others, and being himself instead of trying to copy someone else, he embodied the Mountaintop mindset at its best. The natural human tendency to get others to like us is to try to do what others want and expect of us. But the irony (and beauty) of life is that people will like and respect you MORE if you are uniquely and independently you – especially in the long-run.

If you compromise your values in the short-run, you may get some short-term artificial gains. But I promise you that this way of living will not sustain you in the long-run. Short-term thinking will ultimately leave you feeling empty and hollow.

If you find yourself wanting to copy others or do something to fit in, please don't be too hard on yourself. We've all been there. I just want you to be more aware of that tendency and then actively replace the doubt with feelings of worthiness to fully be yourself in each and every moment.

You can be yourself by reflecting in a journal at the end of each day and identifying your strengths, weaknesses, and areas where you could use improvement. Journaling was critical to getting me out of the setbacks I experienced while in high school. It was a safe medium to vent my unfiltered thoughts and feelings.

The second aspect to Dananjaya's brilliance is developing the student mindset. The best leaders are students first, teachers second. There's always going to be lots of competition in your field while you seek excellence. It is not uncommon to have the next and best person coming up right behind you. The way to stay ahead of the game and maintain your success as you reach for greater heights is to always be learning. People who master their craft don't claim to be gurus – they claim to be students of what they want to master.

Learn from others by asking good questions and listening intently. To embody the Mountaintop mindset, you must come into the present and learn to control the many thoughts in your head. Dive fully into what others are saying. You don't have to integrate everything someone else says into your daily life if it doesn't resonate with you, but at least consider their point of view. Leaders with the Mountaintop mindset know how to listen to others and make other people feel like a million bucks. Take the focus off of yourself and put your attention on learning from others through in-person conversations, books, audio CDs, and the like. Reading a book allows you to take a deep-dive into the psyche of the author (take for example the first chapter of this book where I shared my deepest, darkest secret with you, for your benefit).

One caveat: while learning, don't burn yourself out. Put on the radio and listen to music if you've had enough of the audiobook. Try fiction instead of nonfiction if you are cramming your brain with too much self-help. Again, a huge theme of this chapter is not for you to rigidly think in terms of black and white, but rather to become aware of aspects of the Mountaintop mindset so you can apply them to the situations you encounter. Do what works for you.

Dananjaya has maintained an incredible level of success because he is always learning from others. Humble and easygoing, he doesn't try to impress or show off. He is genuine and has attracted success by the person he became. As he talked about in his award-winning Championship speech, he certainly has had his fair share of ups and downs, but he surrounded himself with the right people –

people who saw something in him and encouraged him to fulfill his greatness – and while he continued to learn and grow, he slowly but surely released his doubts and realized what he has to offer this world.

By *being* a champion and continuing to learn even after he achieved great success, Dananjaya is the perfect example of the Mountaintop mindset. Put yourself out there even when the doubts come or others don't approve of you and watch as the magic starts to unfold.

Flip the whole game on its head. When the doubts surface, use them as signals to move forward and step into the heart of each doubt itself. I know that sounds paradoxical and counter-intuitive, but it's a success strategy that has worked for countless people. Terrified of public speaking? Get up in front of people and speak. Afraid to reveal your true self to the world? Take off your mask and be yourself with every person you encounter.

The irony is that the more you are yourself, the more you encourage others to be themselves. The more you are yourself, the easier you will attract the right people into your life.

There are always going to be setbacks, challenges, delays, unexpected trials, and mistakes. But if you keep in mind some of the core principles of the Mountaintop mindset and then do your best to live them each and every day to the best of your ability, you will skyrocket your chances of reaching your own version of success instead of living someone else's life.

"Success is not in the money you make, but in the fears you overcome," Dananjaya said. By being a person who is focused on overcoming fears, you will have the mindset necessary to help others and become successful.

One more bonus tip from one of Dananjaya's YouTube videos: don't worry if you haven't come into your prime yet. People bloom at different times in their lives. This resonates with me SO much because I was the epitome of a late bloomer. If someone is doing better than you right now, use it as added motivation to improve, but don't get hung up on it – it just means that your best days are ahead of you.

As Brian Tracy says, "No one is better than you and no one is smarter than you. Whatever anyone else has done, within reason, you can do, too. If someone is doing better than you, it's only temporary, not permanent."

My interpretation of this quote by Tracy is not to view life as some crazy competition with others, but rather to view life as an endless opportunity to do amazing things. Don't get intimated by other people's success: as I learned from Tracy's audio programs, everyone who is currently at the front of the line of life was once at the back of the line of life. The key to getting what you want is to get in line and then stay in line. That's what Dananjaya did, and through years of effort and persistence, he made it to the top. He never gave up and is now a huge inspiration to many. When you stay determined and focused on what you can control, you will move beyond obstacles and become one of the best people in your industry of choice.

Learn From Anyone and Everyone

To emphasize just how important it is to always be learning, let's briefly hear from author and blogger Nick Thacker who will speak with us later in the book at greater length:

"From college professors to business mentors, supportive friends to family members, just about everyone in the world can teach us something. We need to have the mindset and clarity to be able to recognize that. Then we need to have the ability to process it for what it is: free consulting.

"Part of being human, I believe, is wanting more. There's nothing inherently wrong with that either, **until our identity begins to get wrapped up in that**. But passion isn't passion because it's a financial means to something more, it's a passion because you can't NOT do it.

"So when you feel frustrated, beat up, or like your life is running in circles, pause and focus instead on what you have. If you had less of it, would you still be happy? How much would you need to lose before you realize how much you actually had? This isn't just a philosophical exercise. Many of us have more than we need, and we all know that money doesn't buy happiness outright."

This is important to hear. Furthermore, Nick touches on two additional key elements of the Mountaintop mindset: always be grateful by counting your blessings, and remember that money is only one small aspect of success.

Money is definitely *not* the only measure of how well you are doing. I emphasize this because money is so thoroughly ingrained into our culture that most people have forgotten what really matters. While money is an important tool to grow your impact, it's not something to become obsessed with.

"Hardly anyone has money to start out, but the good news is that you don't need any," Nick said. "If you want to make an impact in the community, go do that. Volunteer your evenings and weekends helping others, teach a college course, or something of that sort. Write about it on a free blog and make an effort to keep at it."

Don't fall into the trap that you need a certain amount of money to be happy; you can be happy now. There are so many aspects and dimensions to your life that if one area is lacking, there are other areas where you have opportunity. No money, but lots of time? Then find creative ways to help others without spending money. Lots of money, but no time? Then find a cause you believe in and donate. The means will vary from person to person and situation to situation, but there is nearly always a way you can make a difference today if you really want to.

Geeta's Aha Moment

I must share with you professional speaker, writer, and freelancer Geeta Nadkarni's Aha moment because it's a great complement to what Nick said and perfectly embodies everything we're discussing. I first met her in Washington, D.C., at the National Speakers Association conference in July of 2015. She had a 5-minute segment speaking in front of thousands of fellow speakers and absolutely NAILED it, really showcasing her expertise. She did so well in her 5-minute spotlight session that a bunch of businesses and tons of people approached her afterward. This goes to show you that preparation can really pay off.

Geeta was excited for me to share her content in this book. Her mindset, philosophy, and insights tie perfectly into the theme of defining your own version of success instead of letting someone else define it for you. We spoke on the phone for a while after the conference, and I was able to soak in her wisdom. She got her first paid writing gig at 12. While growing up in India, she always had the entrepreneurial mindset.

"I give myself a breather on weekends," Geeta said. "My aha moment was in realizing that happiness comes first – happiness is a decision. Happiness comes first, success comes second. I'm not waiting for the one million dollars to be happy."

"That's very powerful," I said, "and reminds me of what my friend, Michael Benner, says about happiness, (an emotional intelligence expert who will be featured in a chapter after yours in my book)."

"Yes," Geeta said, "it's a great mindset. I'm always living in gratitude with every meal I eat. I also make sure to have way more positive comments in my household than negative ones. Because when you are around negative people, it's a lot harder to maintain the right mindset.

"My 3-year-old keeps me on track," Geeta continued. "If I'm ever mixing up my priorities, my 3-year-old will let me know immediately. I make sure to be LIVING what I teach others. I keep myself tied to what's really important. Far beyond revenue and the daily stuff we get obsessed with, I *make* the decision to be happy. The end."

Geeta is awesome, isn't she? She reminds us that we are always making some kind of choice and happiness can also be a choice. She also touches on the hallmark of the Mountaintop way of life: living and practicing what you teach others. You can't always control what happens to you, but you can control how you respond to what happens to you.

"It's also important to know that when you become successful, a new level of complexity opens up," Geeta said. "So success is really not a destination. I'd like to emphasize the importance of enjoying today. If you enjoy every moment, then you win in every moment. If I'm really stressed, I'll walk away.

"I work out 6 times a week, and I'm very deliberate about making sure my body is in good shape because it keeps my mind sharp. I wake up at 4:30 AM every morning, and it's a total privilege to be able to do this. There are times when it's really bloody hard, and I have to work ridiculously hard, but I enjoy it.

"Work is not so much about sacrifice and tradeoff as it is about purpose and serving others," shared Geeta. "When I'm living on purpose, I feel lit up. That's when I enjoy the rush of creating something from nothing. I also use accountability partners to keep me on track.

"I also meditate all the time, which keeps my mind clear. I average two audiobooks a week. I cut off the safety net and just jumped. I had to replace all the negativity in my life with positive reinforcement. Entrepreneurship is a very lonely journey, and I had to replace 90% of my friends.

"Those who tell good stories rule the world," Geeta continued. "The quality of your life is determined by the quality of your questions. Everything – your relationships, your food, your daily life – it's all about the story you tell yourself. Whatever story you tell yourself will be your reality.

"If you think marriage sucks, it will be a reality. If you tell yourself you can do anything, you can do anything. So it's beyond blogging, it's beyond just doing stuff; it's being super-vigilant about the stories you tell yourself in *every* area of your life. If you don't like the story you are living, then get out your Sharpie and rewrite it," Geeta emphasized.

Geeta, just like all the other champions I've mentioned in this chapter and will refer to later in this book, is the real deal. Even if you're not an entrepreneur, Geeta's lessons are powerful. The final aspect of the Mountaintop mindset is to be willing to reinvent yourself when you're not happy with your current story. Rather than beat yourself up, take the enlightened advice of Geeta and simply decide to paint a new picture. It's not always easy, and it takes time, but this mindset will give you the perfect starting point to live your best life.

Geeta freely acknowledges that the journey is not always easy, and there will be challenges. But if you apply the right mindset and become conscious of your stories, you can write the next chapter in your life with purpose, power, and conviction. This is another powerful and important aspect of the Mountaintop mindset.

There's Always More
Internationally-renowned bestselling author and professional speaker Randy Gage mirrors what Geeta said.

"When you solve one problem, another problem opens up," Randy said. "That's the meaning of life. There are always more challenges, more obstacles, and more problems that will come your way.

"Rather than be discouraged by this, learn to embrace the process," Randy continued. "The only people with no problems are the ones with tombstones above them. Don't create an imaginary finish line. Instead, realize that it's an ongoing and never-ending journey.

"The moment you achieve one goal, you will have a new goal. Success is not linear – there are constant peaks and valleys, ups and downs, wins and losses. As you climb your ladder, make sure you are committing to the right things and treating people the right way."

Randy is loved and admired by many for a reason – he shares brilliant insights, and he's often right. He says that you must be sure to commit to things you truly want to do. The Mountaintop mindset is realizing that even if you are not yet at your goal, you are a champion in each moment by sticking to your values, moving forward, and being the best version of yourself that you can be. And as you rise, remember to treat others with loving-kindness and respect – something Randy embodies amazingly well. If you embrace the important aspects of this mindset, you will be well prepared to implement the strategies in the chapters to come.

Randy introduced me to Scott Dinsmore, founder of Live Your Legend, through one of Randy's periscope sessions. Very sadly, Scott tragically died while climbing Mount Kilimanjaro in September of 2015. He was just 33 years old. Let me leave you with Scott's powerful words taken from his TEDx talk, *How to find and do work you love*, which I'm certain will echo throughout the depths of eternity:

"I did what I loved for four years and didn't make one penny at it, only supported by my parents and wife. What finally made the difference was when I moved to San Francisco and surrounded myself with the right people – people who had the right mindset. Impossible became my new normal."

Questions for Reflection

1. What are some of your recurring negative thoughts? What are some good replacement thoughts for these negative tendencies?

2. In what situations do you particularly beat yourself up? How can you ease up on yourself and become your own best friend?

3. When do you put your happiness off to the future? What can you do to be happy today?

Chapter 3: Be Authentic

"Vulnerability and authenticity lead to genuine success."
– Kathryn Zonghetti

Authenticity is the best way to put the Mountaintop mindset into action. Not only is it pivotal to your success, but it is the perfect setup for the rest of this book.

I was recently speaking to the Students for Professional Advancement (SPA) and Empowering Dreams for Graduation and Employment (EDGE) groups at Central Connecticut State University, and I started the talk by discussing the crucial importance of being authentic. There is nearly nothing that will shortchange your endeavors faster than being someone you are not, and there is nearly nothing that will help you more than to be fully and authentically yourself and who you were meant to be.

I certainly have flaws and shortcomings, but one thing I have going for me is that people say I'm authentic. Being authentic allows me to make *real* connections with other people. I genuinely care about them and seek to help them, as opposed to the hidden agenda so many people carry. You can (and will) absolutely get paid for helping others, but you must make it your first priority to have a sincere interest in the welfare of yourself and the people around you.

This does not mean you will let people use you, nor does it mean you will be afraid to sell yourself on your true value. Being authentic helps to know when to draw boundaries and stand up for yourself. You refuse to be fake. Do you want to be truly authentic? Then make a firm inner decision to do so, right now.

A Perfect Example

A perfect example of authenticity at its best is Jenn Scalia, one of the top business coaches in the world. While succeeding in the entrepreneurial world and growing her business, she put on a few more pounds than she would have liked. This happens to the best of us. In one of the best blog posts I've ever read, she shared her story and how she didn't feel she was her ideal figure (as so many people feel, men and women alike).

Jenn felt overwhelmed with some of the stresses of life, and while doing well in certain areas, she didn't take care of her health and general well-being as much as would have been ideal.

Society, television, and seductive advertisements brainwash us with the idea that maintaining a perfect weight is easy. But for many people, it's not easy at all. The point here is not to talk about the bad information society teaches us from an early age, as that's a topic for another book. Nor is it to talk about weight loss. The point here is to reveal the enormous value of authenticity and how it ties into your ongoing success.

In Jenn's blog post, she revealed that as much as she was putting herself out there, she was still hiding in some ways. In a follow-up post in the same year, she also discussed giving away too much for free and letting other people use her, which is something I've done myself on countless occasions but am actively working to improve. These discussions were powerful because she was helping people to understand that everyone struggles with these challenges, even successful people.

It takes a lot of guts to show your authentic, true self to the world like Jenn did and continues to do. When you do, it not only helps others but also sets you free. Once you do something like Jenn did, there is nothing left for you to run or hide from. As Jim Morrison said, "Expose yourself to your deepest fear; after that, fear has no power, and the fear of freedom shrinks and vanishes. You are free."

When you courageously reveal what's going on in your inner life to the world, you accomplish a number of things:

- You inspire others to do the same, encouraging them to stop hiding in their darkness.
- You develop a supportive, loving community that is there to help you work through whatever it is you're going through.
- You initiate change through a ripple effect in both yourself and others.
- You authentically share a message coming from your true self, and you spread a message that will echo throughout eternity.
- You feel at peace in knowing that in a world where so many people are afraid to be who they really are, you had the awareness and empowerment to be who you really are – sharing the good AND the bad.

Now, I'm definitely not saying to spill your beans to any stranger on the street. Continue to use your best judgment and listen to your intuition as to who you are going to trust. I'm just saying that when it comes to authenticity, be who you really are and not anyone else. There are times when I'm speaking in front of thousands of people when I comfortably share my deepest, darkest moment, and there are times when I wouldn't want to share my story with the one or two people around me. Choose the right moment, but don't be afraid to share. Play to your authenticity and let people see the real you in its entirety.

What if Jenn was too afraid to share her true self with the world? Then many people wouldn't have been enlightened by her example. Sharing with others the thing you are afraid to share lets the light into your situation.

As you build your community, share your story, get out there more, and make your own unique contribution to the world, remember to always be authentic. So many good things come from being your true self and you will love how you make genuine connections from being real and transparent. You have nothing to hide – you are here on the planet to help others while being true to yourself.

Don't Overcommit

Chris Salem is a keynote speaker, life coach, nutrition specialist, leadership expert, and master networker. His strategies will help you to be more aware of the choices you have, live a happier and healthier life, and speak from the heart in all of your interactions with others. I sat down to meet with Chris at a Starbucks in Newtown, Connecticut, the town where I grew up.

We immediately discussed our hectic schedules. We were glad to see one another and at the same time laughing about how we barely have any free time. One of the keys to achieving your own version of success is to stop overcommitting yourself. And when you do commit yourself, make sure you are doing something you really want to do. Being authentic doesn't mean pleasing everyone. It means being clear on who you are and staying true to your values in any and all situations. Make time for the right people, but don't commit yourself to the wrong people and situations.

If you are overcommitting to something you truly enjoy, then that's not really overcommitting: it's enjoying life. But my tendency, as a people-pleaser, often causes me to overcommit. The good news, though, is I'm improving at saying no to others and so can you. This is the hard part of authenticity, but it's a learnable skill.

So HOW do we shed our fear of saying no to people? If you're anything like me, you don't want to just learn why something is important, but how to do it. The answer is detachment.

Chris describes himself as a "prospeneur" who runs an affiliate marketing and networking business. He is also a life, wealth, and health coach. His success comes from his incredible drive to help others. Please keep in mind that this is not "yeah, I love helping others, but really I only care about myself." What is so truly outstanding and mesmerizing about Chris's personality is that he *genuinely* helps others in any way he possibly can, with no expectation of reciprocation. I gravitate towards genuine people, and this is no exception.

"You've got a great presence," I said to Chris. "I love chatting with you; I feel like I'm with my uncle or something. This is great."

"Thanks, Jeff," Chris said. "I appreciate that. It all boils down to detachment. If you come from relaxation and ease, it will actually make people not only want to be around you more but to do business with you. I kid you not, I get more coaching clients than you would ever believe by just relaxing, being myself, and genuinely trying to listen and help others. Too many people are jumpy and filled with expectations, which pushes people away. But if you are one hundred percent YOU, people will sense that relaxation and an energetic connection will occur because you're detached from the outcome."

"Is this the best way to be authentic while saying no when necessary?" I asked.

"Yes. If you are negative in your head, that energy is pushed into your interactions with others. People can distinguish between authenticity and fakeness of short-term gain more easily than you may think. And people appreciate straightforwardness. Come from the point of being confident, relaxed, and at ease. Operate from this mindset and you'll build better connections with people than you could have ever imagined," Chris said.

It's Not Easy: The Understatement of the Century

Adding my own insights here, that's why so many people are inauthentic. It's not like they're trying to be. Most people have good intentions and are doing the best they can. But when their heads are filled with negative thoughts all day, it's no wonder they sometimes come off as mean, calloused, or fake. They are too focused on the negatives. In addition, some people are pure fakes, and they are to be avoided entirely.

Growing up, I would sometimes hear teachers say, "Don't be negative. Be positive!" And I would roll my eyes every time. But as I matured and evolved, I realized that being negative ties into being inauthentic. After learning this, I did everything in my power to break my habit of negative thinking. While not all my teachers were good, it turns out many of them were right after all.

Being positive isn't easy. Truth be told, most days it felt downright impossible. Forget about two steps forward and one step back – it really felt like one step forward, seven steps back. And that negative progression was on a good day. But I kept fighting for something better. I kept looking for that silver lining, even when I couldn't find it. I kept battling my tendency to want to criticize, condemn, and complain. It was a long, slow, arduous, and downright painful process. I did everything in my power to get my mind off of the bad stuff. Meditation. Notecards. Phone calls with family members and friends. Long, reflective walks. You name it, I probably did it. And you know what? It was a sloppy and difficult process. But on the other side of all of these efforts is fearlessly showing your authentic self to the world.

Change is painful in the beginning but becomes easier as you go.

If you haven't been as authentic as you'd like in the past, don't worry about it. You can change your thought processes and habits to reflect who you really are, starting today.

That's what this book offers: the next step. A deep dive. A real, hard look at the way things really are and a process to move beyond the dysfunction. To become genuinely confident and your own person, you must embrace and apply the *Reach Your Mountaintop* process to your life at every step and turn.

Now, this does not mean to avoid or disregard the negative. It simply means to consciously shift and replace the negatives with something better. For example, during my school years, my sports life was literally a disaster. No joke, I could take the story from the first chapter and turn it into a 200-page book with all the unexpected twists and turns. But rather than share a sob story that neither of us really cares about at the moment, let me boil it all down to this: when I focus on the GOOD that came from those bad situations, such as what I learned, the serendipity that came from it all, and the friends I made, I feel peace in knowing that everything happens for a reason. As the late, great Susan Jeffers said, "Even though you may not be able to see it in the moment, it's all happening according to the Grand Design."

Sometimes Susan's quote may be the last thing in the world you want to read. I get that as much as anybody. But if you use this framework as a general compass, you'll more easily find the silver lining and hidden benefit in the difficult situations life presents you with.

You Don't Control Other People, You Only Control Yourself

Let's get back to my conversation at Starbucks with Chris, as he offers us so much.

"I saw your YouTube video in which you talk about getting away from the wrong people and bringing the right kind of energy into your life," I said.

"Right," Chris said. "Glad you saw that. I'm generally a relaxed person. But when I get around my ex-wife, I become jumpy and anxious. When someone is anxious and filled with chaos, it makes you uncomfortable around them. You can either absorb or repel others' energy. However, life will be a lot easier if you get around the right kind of energy and absorb it."

"But what if someone who you thought has good energy betrays you or does something ill-mannered?" I asked. "For example, I've had close friends stab me in the back before, and some people have spoken badly about me behind my back."

"You have no control over somebody else's actions," Chris said. "Why put that stress on yourself? Go with the flow and let go of the control. Let go of the control and life will flow. It all goes back to the continual practice of detachment."

Chris helped me to embrace one of the paradoxes of life. Life is filled with contradictions. And it is up to each one of us to embrace these contradictions in our own way. The more we let go and detach, the easier success will come. We all know success is NOT easy, and it takes hard work, dedication, and positive habits. However, when we remind ourselves to have fun and detach from the outcome, life flows more easily. This is one of the keys to letting go of doubt, achieving our goals, enjoying life, and just being ourselves.

Balancing Ambitious Friends with Not-So-Ambitious Friends

I've often heard it said to completely cut ties with people who are no good for you. While this is the best course of action in some cases, it's not usually necessary. Chris helped to bring this paradigm back into balance for me and hopefully he can do the same for you. Yes, you must get around the right people, but you can also let loose every once in a while.

"Just because someone is not a go-getter doesn't mean you have to cut them off," Chris said. "If they're not completely toxic, it's alright to hang out with them and continue to be yourself. Just manage your time effectively around them. Spending too much time with people who are not in the flow or in a success mindset will hold you back. But there is something called Friday night."

I laugh. Chris chuckles and continues, "My suggestion is to spend 80% of your time with successful people and 20% your time with the others. The problem is that most people have it backward."

"I get what you mean, Chris. If someone absolutely needs to cut another person off, then they can cut them off, but the vast majority of the time there's no reason to burn a bridge. Can you talk more about what you mean when you say 'success' and 'successful people', and how that ties into this crucial foundational concept of authenticity?" I asked.

"Yes, absolutely," Chris said. "Success is not just about the money. When I say success, I'm talking about ethics, trustworthiness, and happiness. Much more importantly than money, success is tied to one's character and general life attitude."

"Yes, I'm following you," I said. "There is much more to success than just money. Too many people seek solely financial rewards and payoffs, and that's why they end up unhappy. Very powerful stuff here. But I must say – doesn't the world revolve around money? Don't most people have some kind of hidden agenda? Isn't it easier said than done?"

"Of course," Chris said. "You ask the right questions, and I love that about you. Now we're really getting into it, and that's the name of the game. Practicing what you preach and applying what you learn. I've met wealthy millionaires who were miserable, and I've met teachers with an average salary living in an average home who were the happiest people you'll ever meet. I'd rather be around the happy teacher. In my book, they're the more successful one because of the authenticity behind their actions."

Did you follow that part of the conversation? Chris is saying you need to shift your mindset to understand that success does NOT stem from money. Money will simply reveal more of what you already are; that's why putting your authenticity first is so important. Yes, pay the bills – and by all means make as much money as you can so that you can expand your influence and help more people in the world – but please don't ever think money is all there is.

"The reason why so few people are successful is because they say one thing and do another," I said. "This is the core delusion of success. People think that successful people can do whatever they want and get away with more things than the average person. What they don't realize is that people only get to where they are because of YEARS of staying connected to their values, being authentic, and taking one step at a time by putting one foot in front of the other. Want to put yourself in the elite few? Then be a person of your word and follow through on your promises. And if you haven't found what excites you in life yet, don't worry, it happens to the best of us – but don't quit. Refuse to give in. Keep on looking for that something and you will find it."

"Very well said Jeff," Chris said. "I mentioned that it's important to have 20% of your time a week given to relaxing, downtime, and having fun. This percentage will vary from week to week, and the optimal percentage will vary for each person, but it's essential that *most* of the time you put up boundaries with people who don't have your best interests at heart; when you're in that mindset of constant personal development and getting to the next level, you need to detach from the average person and get around people who are doing just as good as you are if not even better."

"This is powerful stuff Chris," I replied. "Thanks for sharing all of this. Today was a good day, and I somehow feel lighter and more focused."

For the record, there is absolutely no judgment of others here. There's a difference between judging someone and choosing to step away from them.

Everything is a Choice

As the conversation continued, Chris and I began talking about life choices, something everybody is inevitably faced with. Chris is more conscious than the average person, in the sense that he has tapped into higher levels of awareness when it comes to making more of the right kinds of choices.

When I asked Chris about life choices, he said, "Anything and everything in life is a choice. A negative thought may come, but you choose what to do with it. When someone cuts you off or tailgates you in traffic, you have a choice as to how you will respond. When it comes to choosing your own state of being, you must first BE what you want to experience in the world."

"Please explain further," I said.

"I mean become the man or woman you are looking for," Chris responded. "The great law of reality and life, if there is one, is that you attract what you are. That's why it's so important to make the right kinds of choices, because you will attract people making similar kinds of choices. We all have insecurities and anxieties; that's an unavoidable and normal part of the human experience. But it is solely each person's responsibility to *consciously* change their thoughts, words, and actions on a daily basis."

To expand on what Chris is saying here, we all are going to slip up. We all are going to have setbacks, disappointments, and temporary defeats. But if we follow Chris's words of wisdom, and remember that we are choosing our responses to life, we will be better able to handle life's ups and downs on our journey to the Mountaintop.

You heard me say it once, and I'll say it again: this is YOUR Mountaintop, YOUR journey, YOUR definition of success, and no one else's. I can't emphasize this enough because the moment you become overly concerned with other people's opinions, you lose. Instead, *choose* to use the criticism from others as added motivation to be your best. That's Mountaintop living at its finest.

Someone I interacted with, who shall remain nameless, didn't support me writing this book and probably thought it wasn't the best use of my time. I let it act as added motivation to finally get this book project completed and out into the world. Seeing that people are still living other people's lives, I know this message is needed.

Chris is an inspiring and wonderful man of integrity – I say that sincerely, from the bottom of my heart and soul. I hold my head high, and I continue to treat people in the world with kindness and respect, even when I am not returned the favor. Chris taught me the value of being authentic, even when other people don't return the favor.

What makes you authentic? Think about it and reflect on it, both in your mind and on paper. Knowing these core qualities about yourself will serve you well when you do a deep dive into your soul later in the book. For me, what makes me authentic is that I am a man of my word. In every sense of the phrase, I live this to a tee. I owe no one any money, and I always follow through on my promises. If I promise someone something, I follow through. On the rare occasion that an emergency interferes with an appointment, I apologize profusely and make it a point to reschedule. I don't leave anyone hanging high and dry, and I'm a genuine, true friend.

I also always make sure to return favors to people. If someone introduced me to a connection that helped with my business, I'll do the same or something similar for them. If someone does something to help me, I'll do something to help them.

I get frustrated when people don't always follow through on their word. "You have to understand that not everyone shares your values," my girlfriend wisely told me. With that said, I'm glad that I'm so careful with my word. Not everyone is like this, so it makes me authentic. What is it about you that makes you stand out? What qualities do other people admire in you? Nurture these qualities because they are your base camp foundation as you head for your summit.

Embrace the Process

I first saw Jenny Drescher speak at the Hartford Springfield Speakers Network group up in Windsor, Connecticut. And – you guessed it – I was absolutely blown away by her authenticity. Her deeply caring, intensely passionate, and fully lovable self came across immediately, and I was hanging on her every word.

She told me how she used to be the weird kid, the oddball, the one who didn't fit in. She heard over and over again that she must "always follow the rules." It took many years of change and reflection, but she transformed herself from a rule-follower to a rule-breaker. In the past, she was always telling herself limiting stories, but she has completely changed all that, and now she helps others do the same through coaching, speaking, and facilitation.

"If a rule doesn't work for you," Jenny said, "figure out what does. Don't be mean or disrespectful, just do what works for you on your terms. Be revolutionary if you need to. Someone will be glad you did. Be bold, be audacious – that's where your power and real self lies waiting."

I mention Jenny here because she is very strong and she's the perfect person to tie all of this together. Here are four of her tips:

1. Get really clear about where you put your energy. Monitor your schedule more closely so that you can block out time and achieve the things that are important to you. When your mind is distracted and unfocused, you will have a hard time bringing your whole self into each moment. And you need your whole self to be authentic.

2. Eliminate distractions. People aren't so much intending to hurt and blow off other people as they are living in distraction. Lives are wasted sitting in front of televisions and social media screens (this mirrors Daniel Midson-Short's tip from his awesome speech in Malaysia I was able to see, which is to be present with the people you are with instead of constantly looking at your phone). There is nothing wrong whatsoever with television and social media as long as it's done consciously and in moderation.

3. Learn to say no. At first it feels uncomfortable, but the more you do it, the easier it will get. Remember that every time you are saying yes to one thing, you are saying no to something else. If you are fired up about something then definitely don't be afraid to say yes to it, but also beware of the "should's" and "have to's" that prevent so many people from achieving greatness. They used to stop Jenny as well, but now they no longer have any power over her and the same can be true for you. Being authentic means being kind to others and it also means being true to yourself by saying no to others when and where necessary.

4. Laughter can go a long way in getting out of your own way. Laughter and play. If you feel stuck, go play. Do something that makes you happy, and lose track of time. You'll find yourself naturally feeling more authentic.

Jenny really hits the nail on the head with this deceptively simple, yet incredibly powerful four-step process for bringing your full authentic self to every area of your life.

"Follow the ENERGY," Jenny says. "I know it sounds a little kooky, but it works. What hits you in the gut the hardest? Money and fame aren't good reasons to follow something. Don't fulfill someone else's expectation; follow your gut and listen to your inner wisdom. Usually, there's a little whisper or voice inside that knows better.

"Go back to that which you are naturally drawn to. People have to make choices from their heart, not from their head. We get in trouble when we are too much in our heads."

What Jenny is saying here is that when you do something you are drawn to *even if only for a few minutes a day* you will be happier, healthier, and more authentic. Happiness is the way to your goal! Don't think that someday you will be happy; you can be happy today.

"I love this," I said. "And what if we find it hard to be authentic, like on negative days when our energy level is down, we feel frustrated, and things aren't going our way?"

"We all have those days at times. The thing to remember is everything happens in perfect time, even when it doesn't seem like it," Jenny said. "And there is no failure. I always tell my clients to celebrate failure because failure is just as important as success."

Jenny knows the struggle. She balanced a corporate job for many years while growing her business. She also knows what it's like to be treated poorly by others. Yet now she's an inspirational leader and role model just like Jenn Scalia and Chris Salem.

She had to make sacrifices, move closer to work to buy herself more time, and even reduce her exercise time to find/create more time in her day. She knows that you probably won't be able to live your dream schedule right away. But that authenticity, that purpose, that power that Jenny embodies so well stems from drawing yourself back to what makes you tick.

Are you feeling the good vibes yet? Put your inner life first and watch everything else flow in divine order.

Concluding Thoughts for the Third Chapter

I want to tell you something, my friend. I know there are going to be times when it's challenging to be authentic, either because you are around jerks, or you are around people you simply don't feel comfortable being around. I know the feeling – I wasn't exactly buddies with most of my high school and college baseball teammates (sorry to say, but sports can be very difficult because of the bullying and judging). There are going to be days when your energy drops, and the last thing you want to think about is making an impact – I know that feeling all too well. We all know this feeling and anyone who tells you they don't know this feeling is most likely lying.

"Everyone, even the most the most successful people, have bad days and experience setbacks," Chris Salem said to me on the phone the other day when I told him of a setback I was experiencing. "If someone tells you that they never have any bumps in the road, they are lying to you."

The difference is that when I have those bad days, I come back the next day bigger and better than before. This is where I went wrong in the past and where I'm going right today; it's not about the bad days because we all have those. It's about how you come back from those bad days. It's not what happens to you; it's how you respond that counts.

What does this authenticity have to do with achieving more and making your mark on the world? Everything. It's the core foundation of true success. It's the backbone of dealing with challenges and setbacks in a healthy and life-affirming way. And it's the framework on which you can rest your soul regardless of what other people think or say about you. If you fall back and don't always feel like you are being your authentic self, DON'T BEAT YOURSELF UP. Stay calm, regroup, and come back tomorrow better than you were today. That's Mountaintop-level living at its best.

Questions for Reflection

1. What is a negative situation you experienced in the past? What are the lessons you learned from that setback and how can you share these insights to help others?

2. What is your deepest, darkest fear? How can you face that fear, with the help of others if need be, one step at a time?

3. When do you feel the need to control other people? What are some ways you can reclaim and live your authentic self?

Chapter 4: Be an Unconventional Leader

People will judge you no matter what you do.
So why even care what other people think?
– David Szymanski

As you work on establishing a rock solid foundation to fall back on even when times get tough, it's essential to remember that you will have moments when you don't feel great. But when you think of yourself as a leader, regardless of your present circumstance or situation, you will be implementing into practice a mindset of serving others and staying humble.

The moment I felt like I made progress, my insecurities would rush back. The moment I finally started feeling confident for once in my life, someone would laugh at me, and I'd start feeling bad about myself again. On many days, I did not feel I'd be able to ever make substantial progress.

I share this for several reasons. One, I don't want you to get frustrated or mad at yourself if you apply some of these tactics, and then you fall back into your old ways. It happens to the best of us. When you fall back, the goal is to more quickly remember that things will be alright. The more you beat yourself up for falling back and making mistakes, the longer you will stay down.

The catch-22 here is when you replace self-doubt with self-love and ease up on yourself, you make progress more quickly. You will, of course, continue to hold yourself to high standards and be your best. At the same time, it means that if you make a mistake or fall short of what you know you are capable of, instead of going back down into the dungeon of despair you will reflect and learn from the situation. Make it a point to look for the silver lining, even when it's difficult to find, and then take action to move forward.

The other reason I share my own challenges with getting out of the darkness is because I want you to know you don't need someone else to call you a leader. You can lead from your current situation. You can be a leader even when you are at the bottom of the totem pole. You can lead even when the last thing you think you can do is be a leader.

You Can Always Lead, Even When You Think You Can't

If I can become a leader, so can you. I mean that sincerely. When I went to Sandy Hook Elementary School and Newtown Middle School, I was the shyest kid in the school. I'm now outgoing.

Throughout 2015, I frequently led meetings at the Hartford-Springfield Speakers Network Group in New England, a group consisting of some of the best authors, speakers, coaches, entrepreneurs, philanthropists, and business owners in the region. Also, through my successful digital marketing career, I've led teams in companies across the United States and Europe. I then transitioned into a career as an author and speaker.

I've also failed countless times. I didn't get much playing time on my college baseball team, but everything is relative; having been cut from my high school baseball team, I could appreciate just *being* on the team even though I was a bench player. Rather than sit around and feel sorry for myself, I decided to root for my teammates, encourage them when they were feeling down from a bad play, give them high-fives, and be an avid supporter.

This may seem inconsequential and like it didn't matter, but most of my teammates appreciated having me around because they knew I brought good energy with me. I wasn't good friends with some of them, but I did have fun stepping on the field with them. Yes, I was incredibly frustrated that the coach didn't give me a shot to play and showcase my minor-league caliber hitting abilities, but I wasn't going to let that keep me bitter since I still had an opportunity to lift my teammates up.

Look for the Hidden Opportunity

With every setback is a hidden opportunity, some kind of silver lining. As a leader, it's important to think about how you can transcend your current situation and move forward.

I was a college recruit athlete and one of the best players in the state of Connecticut. My college baseball coach saw me at a showcase (where top high school players play to impress college scouts and coaches so that they can get recruited to play at a higher level) and I was considered by many people there to be one of the best players on the field.

When it came to hitting, my strongest aspect as a player, I hit more doubles than anyone else on the field. I was crushing the ball and completely in my element.

After that showcase, I got recruited to play at a collegiate level by many schools, including McDaniel College – where I ended up going to school. My college coach didn't even know I got cut from my High School baseball team. He would have been beyond dumbfounded if I told him that happened because I was one of the best players on the field, competing against some of the best high school ballplayers in the nation.

The challenging part of this particular circumstance is that while my college coach started out as a huge supporter, he ended up becoming a critic. Have you ever had someone go from a supporter to a critic in your life? Imagine being close with someone and then having them unexpectedly turn on you. Even though I was a college recruit athlete and one of the best players in the state of Connecticut, I had one bad game in the fall season of my freshman year of college (it happens to even the best ballplayers out there) and my college coach made a split-second decision that I was no good – after that I had many good games in scrimmages, but he didn't seem to take note of my successes. I made the college team, but the coach had an impression of me that couldn't be changed.

A bit unfair, but completely out of my control. At the end of my sophomore year, with a boatload of new recruits coming in, my intuition told me to consider studying abroad. McDaniel's main campus abroad is in Budapest, and I'm 25% Hungarian, so I felt like it was meant to be. I definitely wasn't running away from my college baseball experience – I was consciously entering into a life of adventure by deciding to live more fully.

After really thinking about it and weighing my options, I ended up studying abroad. On my third day there, by serendipity, I found out about a Hungarian baseball team. I tried out, did well, got along with all my teammates, and joined the team.

As the late Randy Pausch, author of *The Last Lecture*, said, "We cannot control the cards we are dealt, just how we play the hand." If I had been a starter, I would have never gone abroad, but I trust everything happens for a reason. And ironically my travels have become the foundation of my entire writing and speaking career. Funny how that works, isn't it? The very thing that I initially thought was an obstacle, delay, detour, and second-best option – not getting any playing time on my college baseball team and going abroad – became one of the best years of my life and the fuel to the fire of my achievement.

I went from a disastrous high school baseball experience, to a less crappy but still terrible college baseball experience, to competing in tournaments across Europe against some fantastic ballplayers, people who were at the minor league level. I didn't let others stop me from doing what I loved.

You can find a silver lining in unexpected, unwanted, and unwelcomed situations. Always look for the silver lining and even when it seems impossible to find, you'll find it if you really look for it. What I've learned from my conversations with leadership experts is that if you look for the good in even really bad situations, you are demonstrating an ability to be an example for others. Leadership is about looking for the silver lining in a challenging situation.

Look for Solutions

Let's now feature input from leadership expert, speaker, and author Heather Hansen O'Neill, who I was chatting with recently at the Newtown diner and featured on my YouTube channel:

"All leadership starts with a sense of self-leadership," Heather said. "It's important to live these principles yourself. It's an ability to believe in something, doing it for the right reasons. You must also come across as authentic and be persistent with your efforts.

"Have leadership over your own emotions. When you know you have a passion which will help people and impact the world, then you know you're doing the right thing, and you'll continue doing the right thing. And like I said, Jeff, you live it," Heather was kind enough to emphasize.

"Wow, that is very powerful," I said. "When it comes to harnessing your emotions and dealing with challenges, are there any tricks you share with others to help them overcome that?"

"Yes, when dealing with challenges," Heather said, "the ability to be quiet is very important. When we have challenges we often have a lot of internal resistance. The ability to sit with that feeling and then transition through it quickly so you can see what the end result could be is very helpful. See if you can figure out what the potential of the situation is and what some of the solutions are.

"Shift your focus by becoming quiet and reducing the internal chaos," Heather continued. "Take the time to see what the possibilities are. Ask yourself: what could be a potential solution to this challenge? Everyone has a situation where they went through a challenge years ago, and they look back at it and go *wow, I learned this strength, and it made me a better person.* Make that leap in your head: *I know I'm going to feel this way at some point, so why not feel this way right now?* If you can go through it now, it will be hugely beneficial."

Heather's words are amazing, to say the least. I love her input here because she hits on a crucial theme of this book: reaching your Mountaintop is nothing more than applying small, practical kernels of wisdom in each present moment. If you don't apply anything, your life won't improve. Start with one small thing – just make sure you start. That's why the best leaders on the planet are the ones who fully embody their own messages.

I've taken it upon myself to live what I'm teaching here, as have all of these experts. By no means am I perfect and I continue to make mistakes, but I've been in the trenches and understand the struggle. It took me more than two decades to learn this. You must find a way to put your knowledge into real action.

If you're not failing and facing rejection every now and then, you're not putting into action what you know.

Here's a great example, speaking directly from my own experience: social media. We all have strengths and weaknesses and while one of my strengths is public speaking, one of my weaknesses is social media. I love being face-to-face with people and seeing their reactions to my messages. The thought of putting something up on the internet without seeing someone's immediate reaction scared me. I especially felt anxiety when no one liked or commented on a particular post.

What I did is I kept on using social media even though it made me feel uncomfortable, because I knew my message could reach more people by sharing it online. I had to get used to the fact that not everyone will always engage with my posts. Some of my Facebook posts got lots of likes, and other posts got little to no likes. Some of my tweets got favorites, retweets, and comments, and other tweets got no response.

The point here is that some of my posts failed – they got little to no engagement. What I learned to do is rather than get hung up on the results of a single post, it's best to put your content out there continuously. *This risks failure, but holds the possibility of helping someone and/or achieving your goal. You must become comfortable with taking risks in order to get what you want and make a real difference in the world.*

I turned a weakness into a strength by failing my way to success. Some weeks my posts failed, but other weeks my posts succeeded. It was through the posts that got no engagement that I learned the value of persistence, maintaining an even-keel, and pushing forward. I also realized that even if a post gets no engagement, it still could have made a positive impact (sometimes people who don't like or comment on any of my posts message me saying they love the content I post).

Now my social media posts get more engagement than they did previously. This doesn't mean I'm an expert at social media, but it does mean I've learned what works and what doesn't. I'm maintaining a beginner's mindset and continually shifting my strategy to make more of a positive impact in people's lives. By facing the fear of rejection and continually learning from my mistakes, I was able to connect with more people. You can do this too.

Another quick example is making a sale. Every rejection and "no" is one step closer to a victory and "yes." The best salespeople are the ones who encounter the most rejection because they are putting themselves out there the most.

If J.K. Rowling let failure and rejection stop her, we wouldn't have the iconic world-renowned Harry Potter series. Rejection is a good thing, not a bad thing, because it means you are putting yourself out there and moving forward. Leaders are scared of failure and rejection like everyone else, but they don't let the fear stop them from putting themselves out there anyways.

Dare to Be Different

Bill Corbett, an author, professional speaker, trainer, friend, and mentor of mine, also has some valuable leadership insights that tie right into the self-leadership Heather told us about.

Bill and I both spoke at a youth leadership conference in early March of 2016 to an audience of eight hundred students – Heather Hansen O'Neill, who we just heard from in the previous pages, is the one who created and hosted the event, bringing Bill and me in as speakers.

I spoke in the morning but stayed to hear the other speakers.

"Leadership is about doing something different than everyone else," Bill said.

Bill talked about the importance of standing out from the crowd and being a leader in many areas of your life.

"Show leadership in your home by getting everyone to sit down in a room at some point in the week and share something going on in their life," Bill said. "It might sound like something you don't want to do, but it's a great way to connect with your family and find out what's going on in their lives."

I love this. Leadership is about stepping outside of the norm and doing something you wouldn't normally do. At first, sitting around chatting with your family, without the distraction of television or electronic devices, may seem uncomfortable. But it will lead to a heightened sense of connection with your loved ones, which will be useful to have when you experience setbacks.

The other aspect I love about Bill's insights into being an unconventional leader is that it doesn't have to be about doing something on a grandiose scale. Yes, that's where you're headed, but start small and work with what's in front of you today. Leadership may mean going to the coffee shop to work on your project instead of going out and drinking alcohol. Leadership may mean strengthening a relationship with your family member by putting the phone down for a half hour instead of endlessly being lost in social media and email.

If you are anything like how I used to be when I heard about leadership, you roll your eyes and think, *oh great, now I have to figure out how to go to Washington, D.C. and speak in front of tens of thousands of people, changing the world*. I've made this mistake as much as anyone else, and I have the frustrations to prove it. But what I've learned is it's not about trying to change everything at once. Think globally, but act locally. Make a small, tiny shift in your habits. Be a little bit kinder. Work a little bit harder. Have a little more discipline. Encourage others and genuinely care about what they're experiencing. Do this and you're genuinely a leader. It's not about changing the world in one fell swoop. It's about leading yourself, being an example for others, and stepping into your unique possibilities one day at a time.

Reaching your Mountaintop is about making daily progress by leading yourself. It's about focusing on the small things within your control rather than the big things outside of your control.

Bill has been through a lot of ups and downs in his life and has persevered through it all. He shows leadership by encouraging and helping others in many different ways. He's a great example of the possibilities that can open up when you focus on leading yourself instead of worrying about what's outside of your control. He also embodies the fact that leadership is more about creating leaders in others than it is having people follow you. Rather than trying to get people to be like you, encourage people to dare to be the quintessential version of their own self!

Next, we will hear from my friend Ann Meacham, also a leadership expert. Before I interviewed Ann about leadership one on one, I had the pleasure of watching her conduct a thorough program on critical thinking skills. Critical thinking is a cornerstone of effective leadership so we will start out with key kernels from her program and then move into the conversation we had with one another.

The Importance of Critical Thinking as a Foundation of Leadership

The first aspect of critical thinking comes down to asking the right questions. When I heard Ann discussing this in her presentation, I got excited because I've always been a question asker and a curious person, someone who wonders about everything (including both the good and bad aspects of life). The secret to knowledge is not to have all the answers, but to ask the right questions.

A good rule of thumb is to question authority figures, people who claim to know it all. Questioning people does not mean you are disrespecting people. Remember, being polite, friendly, and respectable are hallmark traits of successful people. Questioning others just means that you think for yourself.

From my own experience, I can testify to the challenge of blocking out the noise of other people's opinions. Even as an independent thinker, it's *incredibly* easy to fall into the trap of automatically believing the spoken word without questioning it. But Ann gives us a series of practical questions to ask when facing particular statements and claims from others:

1. Who said that?
2. Is that source reliable?
3. Is there data to support that claim?
4. Has it been scientifically proven?
5. Is this person qualified to speak on this topic?
6. Do they have a personal stake in this issue?

"While I grew up," Ann said, "I wasn't very discerning. I took what some people said to be truth."

I loved Ann's transparency and honesty as a speaker, as I am transparent and honest myself. I completely relate to Ann being too trusting while growing up. I far too frequently took other people's words as the truth.

"One time I asked someone where I should park my car," Ann said. "I wanted to put it in my driveway, but the other person said to park it on the road. It ended up being a bad decision because I ended up falling and badly injuring myself. I had to learn to stop listening to other people without checking in with myself first! Sometimes we forget to do this and just out of habit we do what others ask us, even at a self-sacrifice."

Here we have more powerful advice from Ann. Constructive feedback and helpful advice from others are great, but Ann knows we must not let others dictate what to do, especially if it's detrimental to yourself – this is relevant because it is also a key kernel of leadership and leading yourself to your own mountain, your own version of success. You may have initially thought that where Ann parked her car was insignificant, but it ended up costing her a broken wrist and great pain.

Please know that Ann is not blaming the other person for her injury. Rather, she is helping us to become aware of the tendency that we all have, including me, to listen to other's thoughts and opinions before our own. Consider outside feedback and other points of view, but don't betray yourself if your intuition is telling you that you have the right answer.

Sometimes the best leaders are forced to do what's unpopular. As a leader, you must do what you feel to be right even when other people disagree with your decision.

Ann gave another highly relevant example that you might relate to. She was working on a project and wanted other people's opinions, so she asked her friend what she thought.

"My friend wanted me to do what was best for my friend, not for me," Ann said. Put your antenna up and ask: *do they have a stake in the outcome?*"

Ann went on to provide the audience with more useful questions to ask when considering a new idea. It's important to take time to make the right decision, but there's a certain tipping point where more time could be a bad thing.

"The longer it takes to decide something, the harder it gets," Ann said.

To make the decision-making process easier and more effective, Ann encourages us to continually ask the following four questions:

1. What do we already know about this idea/choice in question? What are the pros and cons? Start with what you know and work your way from there.

2. What concerns us? Writing down our concerns helps us to identify bottlenecks, which in turn gives us insight into potential solutions.

3. What scares us? Sometimes writing down our fears, worries, and concerns can be the very thing that helps us to move beyond them. Worst-case scenarios are usually not as bad as we may have initially thought.

4. What could be the benefits? Oftentimes we are so preoccupied with what could go wrong that we forget the possibility of everything working out in our favor (which, as you know, is never guaranteed, but nonetheless far more likely than you may have initially thought and expected).

Critical thinking is a powerful skill. It's straightforward and relatively simple, but not always so easy to apply. The truth is that most people do not ever engage in critical thinking. As Napoleon Hill pointed out in *Outwitting the Devil: The Secret to Freedom and Success*, the sad truth is that most people don't think for themselves. But you are not most people. If you have read this far, then I'm certain you are the kind of person who is destined for great things. I say that not in some airy-fairy romantic sort of way, but rather in a real, genuine, and practical way for you to find your own truth and then act on it.

Once you connect with your own inner wisdom and truth, it will then be a lot easier to help others find theirs.

Leadership at its Best

Now that we have a solid foundation for the fundamentals of critical thinking, we can smoothly transition into my one-on-one conversation with Ann about leadership.

"There are a lot of different opinions about what the most important aspects of a leader are," Ann said. "The basics are that the leader sets the vision, provides the things that the people need – like resources and encouragement – and then provides a framework for those goals to be accomplished. The leader will then hold others accountable for getting it done."

To insert some extremely valuable leadership expertise from author, professional speaker, and prosperity expert Randy Gage, here's one of his periscopes while he was in Florida:

"There are all sorts of books out there with leadership tips from people who've never led anything," Randy said. "Yes, there are some general tips to consider, but ultimately it's about having a vision and then leading people to that vision."

Randy's Mountaintop-level insights are a perfect addition to Ann's points. I love sharing principles with you that are backed by the knowledge and experience of several experts. Later in the book, we will hear much more from legendary entrepreneur Randy Gage, an incredibly inspiring man and a history-maker. I felt compelled to share his insights here because he and Ann see eye-to-eye on what leadership is really all about. Now, back to Ann.

"Those are the three keys," Ann said. "Vision, providing resources, and accountability. On top of that, a leader is also a facilitator. If you are in a meeting, they will facilitate and make sure everyone participates. They convene the meeting and keep everything on track. For example, it's not uncommon for a leader to spend multiple days facilitating with the senior team of a company.

"The leader inspires," Ann continued. "If you go to a leader for help, a true leader will be at your service and do everything they can, within reason, to help you. They use stories and anecdotes to support their claims. For example, I've heard you speak about the beauty, power, and awesomeness of your late Aunt Meg before, Jeff, which is great. You have the right idea with that: you are showing others that they can be inspired the same way you were inspired by your late Aunt."

Weaving in my own input, keep in mind that it takes a large degree of self-discipline and self-leadership to put into action the behavior necessary to turn a vision into reality. Vision is crucial, and without the right behavior the vision doesn't unfold the way it was meant to. Rather than just telling others what to do, lead the way by inspiring others to believe in the vision and make it their own.

Also, show compassion for others by listening to them and showing you care. Show compassion not in theory, but in reality, especially when it's tough to do so. This is not easy to put into action and takes practice, but if you remind yourself of the importance of practical compassion on a daily basis you will become an exceptional leader.

Making the most of my opportunity to chat with Ann and pick her brain, I continued to ask her questions.

"What about leadership as it pertains to motivation?" I asked. "Isn't motivation sort of an overused term nowadays?"

"A true leader never motivates anyone, but rather shows people how to motivate themselves," Ann said.

Piggybacking off of Ann's insightful comment, I'd like to add that motivation isn't about fluff like some people think. Motivation is about looking at one's daily life and then using relevant strategies to continue moving forward. When used and applied effectively, proper motivation can be the difference between success and failure.

It's important to apply this knowledge consistently. Seek to make small changes, and then turn those changes into habits. That's how leaders are made.

The Key

"It's all about having that vision," Ann said. "If you do the right things then you can have what you want. You really need to start with a vision. Goals are more of a to-do list for how to get there."

"That's great," I said. "It makes a lot of sense to start with a vision. Tell me more about goals."

"Goals are success indicators," Ann said. "If it's three years from now and you've reached your vision, setting and reaching goals are the indicators that let you know you're there."

Some examples Ann shared with me:

- Getting hired for [you fill in the blank] number of engagements.
- Getting paid X [you fill in the blank] amount per speech.
- Consistently getting X [you fill in the blank] kind of feedback after a certain task, project, business initiative, etc.
- Defining success for yourself as [you fill in the blank].

Success is about defining what you want on your terms. This is not about what someone else wants for you. This is about what you want for yourself.

"For example," Ann continued, "success for some could be having a booked schedule because they are in demand."

I like how Ann talked about concrete results, and at the same time talked about more subjective aspects of leadership and success. This process involves creating your own framework, so you become a forward thinking leader who knows where you're leading people.

Parting Words

"Remember," Ann said, "leadership is critical in every area of our lives. And when it comes to leading yourself, it's really all about less stress and more peace."

As we wrapped up our discussion, Ann talked about how leadership is not about stressing out all of the time. Be disciplined when it comes to your goals, but consciously give yourself some breathing room as well.

"It's really too bad how many people give their life over to the goals to the point that they are eaten, without ever enjoying life and without really living," Ann said. "Too many people live to work, rather than work to live. That's where balance comes into this discussion as well."

"That's a great point," I said. "For example, I have an upcoming trip to a big conference in California, and I'm doubting whether or not I should have booked the trip. But I'm going for sure now, so I figure I might as well use it as an opportunity to relax. In addition to the conference, I will have one or two days of downtime."

"Of course," Ann said. "Enjoy your trip as much as you can. Conferences are excellent because they give you a chance to learn valuable new material without expending too much energy and still recharge. When we try to do too much, we wear out. Jeff – you're young, you can pull crazy hours and work as hard as you do, but realize that it doesn't take 20 years to burn out. You – and I don't mean you personally, but anyone who is working too hard – could wake up one day and say *I don't care, I don't care, I don't care*. Leadership is also about taking care of yourself."

I *completely* relate to Ann's words of wisdom here. I do work hard, and I am a forward thinker, but I have had many moments where I was so frustrated, burned out, and exhausted that I started not caring about my goals. Even while writing this book, my schedule was so unbalanced that I was starting to lose sleep. This led to waking up feeling frustrated to the point where I cared less about my goals because I didn't have my usual energy during the day. An all-nighter every now and then is awesome (and I *love* that feeling of task-completion, as I'm sure you do as well), but Ann is saying that too many of those nights in a row will catch up to you – and she's absolutely right.

The point here is that leaders establish self-sustaining, productive, and healthy long-term habits, including getting a good night's sleep. When reaching for a vision, they know it's about consistent daily progress, not a one-time sprint.

I successfully counteracted those feelings of not caring by giving myself a break and recharging – now I'm 100% back on track. Rest is crucial.

"People brag about having no vacation days," Ann said. "But that's foolish. I use every vacation day I can.

Vacation helps me to recharge so I can return feeling refreshed. For example, I knew of a CEO of a nonprofit who had a million things going at once. This is particularly common for people who are in charge. She couldn't get a handle on her stress and continuously felt overwhelmed. Even a month off didn't help. She actually took a month off, but still couldn't get away from the stress. She was so overwhelmed she had to quit. Don't let that happen to you – don't let your work burn you out.

"Pace yourself. And have fun! Create relationships with people you meet by following up with them via email and phone. Join a mastermind or networking group of some sort."

My discussion with Ann came at the perfect time because of my upcoming trip to California. During my trip, I made sure to enjoy it while learning new information at the conference. I love how my conversation with Ann spontaneously occurred after she was done presenting; sometimes the best input comes from putting down our worries and just chatting with people. And you know who I got to meet on that trip to California, by pure serendipity? Michael Benner and John Lee Dumas, who we will hear from later in this book.

Take action as often as you reasonably can. Stay super-focused on your vision and goals. Just don't forget to smell the roses along the way! It's up to you to decide exactly what kind of break/balance is appropriate for your particular situation, but please know that it's alright to create some breathing room in your life.

Focus on the important stuff, let the insignificant worries go, and enjoy each and every moment life offers you even before you've reached your end destination – life is just too short to do otherwise. Combine breaks with these leadership tips, and you will be well on your way to reaching your Mountaintop.

Another Powerful Leadership Expert

Let's recap before moving ahead further. Leaders are people who lead from within. They do what's right regardless of the circumstances or if it's an unpopular choice. They have a vision and seek to enlist people in that vision. They also look to *create* leaders by serving others. It's not about getting followers, but rather creating powerful co-collaborators. Leaders are innovative and imaginative, seekers of excellence, authentic, ballsy, focused on daily behavior, and true to themselves.

In addition to Ann, another great example of a leader is entrepreneur and LinkedIn expert Mike Shelah. I had the honor, privilege, and pleasure of grabbing coffee with him in Westminster, Maryland. Mike embodies all of these qualities of leadership and more. He certainly has had plenty of setbacks and disappointments, but he is a wholly positive person and a joy to speak with.

"After making decisions, true leaders are slow to change them," Mike said. "As Simon Sinek, author of *Start with Why*, says, 'Seek to understand yourself and why you made particular decisions.'"

What Mike is saying here is that it's fantastic to pursue opportunities to the fullest, but don't change from one endeavor to another without a reason and purpose for doing so. I have lots of energy, and I'm constantly generating new ideas, but I make sure to stick with a project and see it through to completion. I tend not to jump around by choosing to channel my energy into a specific purpose. When you know why you chose a particular course of action, it will be more difficult for someone to deter you from your path (we all face countless external influences on a daily basis). When you become clear on your why, you can focus your energies on a single, important task.

Be flexible in your approach, but be deliberate about the decisions you make. Give yourself time and don't let others rush you. Once you make a decision, be true to yourself and follow through.

From a leadership point of view, be aware of the "bright, shiny object syndrome" where it is easy to become so excited about new opportunities that you never see your ideas through to completion. Part of the process of becoming the expert yourself is to make a decision and then **make your decision right, rather than endlessly worrying about making the right decision.** This is the brilliance I picked up from talking to Mike.

I can speak to this because I've been there! I have an innate and true love for traveling, so for a while, I was bouncing back and forth between being a travel expert and being a youth (middle school, high school, and college) expert. I finally got sick and tired of the delay of indecision, so I thought, *alright, cool – I've lived abroad, traveled the world, and genuinely had some ridiculously amazing travel experiences. But I'll never be the "go-to" guy in the youth market unless I put my whole heart and soul into it, instead of being half in travel and half in the youth market.*

Guess what happened? High schools and colleges started seeing me as the expert. I've now spoken to youth not only in the United States of America but also in Europe and Asia. But it wasn't an easy process. It took a heck of a lot of leadership because I had to not only be 100% accountable for my thoughts, actions, and habits, but I had to cut out the outside world and listen to what my heart and soul were telling me to do. And you know what the beauty of it all is? I still travel all the time (as I write these words I'm 38,000 feet in the air, traveling home from Europe to the United States). You can have multiple passions, and you can pursue multiple things at the same time. Just be sure to have that one main focus.

Leaders ask themselves: *What do I want the most? And how can what I want the most help others?* Once you have that figured out, then live your values, create a vision, and go after it! It's not always easy to do it in practice, but it's a straightforward process. And it's an *ongoing* endeavor, not a one-time thing.

This is what Mike means when he talks about leadership. When making a decision, make sure to do something for the right reasons. And then align your habits and daily actions to run with your decision. The world favors the bold. Leaders are courageous and go after what they want with full force.

"I took a sales job when I was younger," Mike said, "and I didn't vet it. It turned out to be one of the worst career moves I've ever made. The lesson I learned from that experience is to take a job because it makes you happy, not just for money or one of the million other reasons there are to take a job."

I relate to Mike here because I, too, made the same mistake when I was younger. I got lied to in the interview about what the job would be like, so it wasn't entirely my fault, but the lesson I learned from that experience is that you are vetting the company as much as they are vetting you.

This book is not a job interview handbook, but this was the perfect way to end the chapter: reminding you that leaders make decisions from *within* and *for the right reasons*. This is the essence of reaching your Mountaintop. Of all the different situations you will encounter in your life – good and bad, big and small – this is one of the most important tips to remember. Start with leading yourself by understanding yourself, and knowing why you do certain things. The more you know your why, the less external factors will be able to sway you astray. When you do this, things will start to flow beautifully for you.

Key Aspects of Leadership to Remember
As a quick recap, here are some of the best leadership insights. Any one of these points can change your life for the better:

- Make small, tiny, daily changes.
- Give away the credit and take the blame.
- Serve, encourage, and inspire others in a real, genuine, and practical way.
- Seek not to gain more followers, but to help create leaders in others.
- Act with courage and integrity by doing the right thing even when it's not the most popular or well-received decision.
- Always respect others and treat people with kindness, but don't be afraid to rock the boat if you know you are moving the ball forward and sharing your authentic message.

- Freely share yourself with others – be open, vulnerable, and willing to reveal your anxieties and fears (when the time and situation are right).

- All leadership starts with self-leadership: rather than worrying about changing the world or other people, go to work on yourself. Get so busy improving your own habits, thought processes, actions, and daily activities that you don't even have time to criticize or judge others.

Learn From the Best and Surround Yourself with the Right People

Before we leave this chapter, let me emphasize that good leaders are not only assembling top-notch teams but also surrounding themselves with the right people. We mentioned this tip earlier in the book, but I'll mention it again because it's so important.

My friend, Geronda Wollack, human resources consultant, entrepreneur, and speaker, says she is amazed by the transformation I've made over the last year and a half – I've gone from good to great as a speaker and have evolved fairly quickly in a short period of time. This is largely due to surrounding myself with the right people (amazingly kind, friendly, and smart people such as Geronda). Geronda is an inspiration, always encouraging others and lifting them up – a true leader.

I then go back to these people who have lifted, raised, and inspired me to greater heights. They always tend to say, "I had no part in it. It was all you." To my credit, I did work my butt off to apply what I learned. But to their credit, they are the ones who got me thinking in the right direction. They are just being humble.

You need people who get you thinking in terms of possibility, hope, and accomplishment – people who make you feel like a million bucks. You do need constructive feedback from honest people, but the feedback should never be given to you in a destructive, overly critical way. One of the keys to success and reaching your own Mountaintop is to surround yourself with the right people.

Nick Thacker, a successful blogger and author I briefly mentioned earlier who has assembled an awesome email list and community, says, "It is so true that no one is an island. If I've succeeded anywhere in my life so far, it's been because I haven't been afraid to ask for help or advice. When I meet a business owner, I ask if I can buy them lunch or coffee sometime. You'd be surprised how many times they say yes and how many times those little asks turn into a real friendship or mentorship.

"I recently asked the CEO of one of the top 10 zoos in the world to grab a coffee and he said yes," Nick continued. "Leading up to our one-hour meeting was one of the most nerve-wracking and terrifying weeks in my life: what would we talk about? What if he thinks I'm an idiot? What do I wear? What if he feels our meeting is a big waste of time?

"Turns out I learned a LOT that day and we both had a great time. I listened to stories about business, life, and doing things that matter. We were able to relate to each other on a lot of it. But what I really learned was the power of asking. The worst someone can ever say is no and that should give you comfort. If it doesn't, ask anyway, and get used to hearing no – it's good for you.

"A lot of what I said isn't wise, unique, or even new. But it's true – it takes time, effort, and a lot of hard-earned failures to make something truly valuable as a leader. I'm still working on that myself, and I ALWAYS get sidetracked. But keep your 'eye on the prize', as the saying goes, and focus on what 'success' means to you."

Nick, like Heather, Bill, Ann, Randy, and Mike, embodies the qualities of a leader. Nick has the courage to ask for what he wants and lives with integrity by staying true to his values. He's also very humble and didn't even acknowledge his achievements in our communications. He reached his Mountaintop because he put the focus on serving others. He defined his own version of success, and has done and continues to do incredible things with his life.

Concluding Thoughts

When you are applying some of these tips, insights, and strategies, remind yourself daily that leaders aren't afraid to be themselves and create their own formula of what works for them in their lives. Every day, every hour, sometimes even every minute, the world will try to convince you to be someone you're not. Push back. Push back respectfully and kindly, but never be afraid to push back. There are so many different ways to be successful – choose the way that works best for you!

For example, my author friends tell me just to write. My speaker friends tell me not to worry about writing at all and just speak. My digital marketing friends tell me to forget about writing and speaking and grow my career in the lucrative field of marketing analytics. And my travel friends tell me that I should be solely focused on a travel blog.

What works *for me* is to combine all of these, with a focus on the high school and college markets. It's alright to have multiple passions! It's ok to apply bits and pieces of advice from others without listening to every little thing they say. You are your own person, your own boss, and no one is in control of your life but you. People can help and offer advice. Sometimes the advice they offer is helpful, but in the end, it comes down to you understanding yourself and your needs. That's what self-leadership, and eventually leading others, is all about.

Sometimes you're going to have to ignore the opinions of others. Sometimes you're going to have to detach from the dysfunction going on around you and keep your eyes on that vision instead of the stressed craziness of people who lose their cool for no reason. Just make sure to live what you teach others. Be a person of character and have the same personality with everyone you encounter.

Some people teach principles to others, but then they don't LIVE those principles themselves. Of course, it's a challenge to live the principles, and no one is perfect, but the effort needs to be made daily. Be true to your word and live your message.

Regardless of what others think, say, or do, be a leader and example for others by showing your true self to the world and just GOING for it. You can do it, my friend.

Questions for Reflection

1. Think of a negative or unpleasant situation you experienced recently. What is the silver lining? What is the hidden opportunity in the setback? If what happened was completely out of your control, what can you learn from the situation about yourself?

2. What is the big fifteen-year vision for your life? What is your five-year vision? What is your one-year vision? What is your four-month vision? What behavior will get you to your vision, starting today?

3. How can you lead yourself better? What is one small thing you can do, starting now or tomorrow, to show leadership in your daily life?

Chapter 5: Sustain Emotional Intelligence and Choose an Even-Keeled Response

"The best parts of yourself exist
where you are most afraid to look."
– Michael Benner

This next person I interviewed, Michael Benner, is the perfect person to come next as you climb your own Mountain and create your own version of success because he is one of the world's experts in emotional intelligence. Research shows that emotional intelligence is the number one key indicator of success in the workplace. I recently saw well-known author, speaker, and social media expert, Gary Vaynerchuk, on the *Good Day New York* TV show say that he was a D and F student, but has built a multi-million dollar (and soon to be billion dollar) business with his emotional intelligence as the backbone.

As we establish and expand upon a strong emotional, mental, and spiritual foundation, you will find Michael's words to complement and build upon what we've already talked about quite well.

Michael is in his sixties, and let me tell you: his energy, knowledge, intelligence, and overall demeanor is that of someone in their thirties or forties. A big reason why I wanted to talk to Michael is because of the depth of his expertise. He has spent more than thirty years in the personal development field through radio shows, podcasts, and all sorts of coaching and other programs. He knows the power of understanding yourself. I first found out about Michael from my father who loved and frequently listened to Michael's radio show in Los Angeles, California, for many years.

"It's all about self-awareness," Michael said. "There is an intuitive wisdom in everything that hurts, irritates, and frustrates us. There is an understanding that is enfolded within negative feelings."

Emotional intelligence is a term first coined by Daniel Goleman. In today's fast-paced and hectic world, it's more important than ever.

"In business and in success, an emotional quotient (EQ) is five times more important than an intelligence quotient (IQ). Social skills and how you get along with other people is much more important than your SAT score or your grade transcript from college," Michael said. "Do you know how to shake hands and make eye contact? Do you know how to listen intently, generate charisma, and create magnetism with other people? Do you have the qualities of a leader that would make other people want to follow you and do what you suggest? These are all much more about emotional intelligence than mental intelligence."

"I agree completely," I said. "I received good grades in school, and I have an analytical mind. With that said, I can genuinely say my ability to get ahead in my speaking career has to do with listening to others and creating a connection. Of course, it's not about me, it's about helping others, but I found the irony is that the more I seek to serve others, the more good things come my way. And I'm always learning more from people like you. Would you please dive even further into emotional intelligence and how to develop it?"

"There are two basic parts to emotional intelligence," Michael said. "The first part is to know thyself; to understand the WHY behind your thoughts, actions, and behaviors. We have all heard of the W's: who, what, when, where, why and how. The 'why' is emotional in nature and it tends to be overlooked, but it's a crucial part of the equation of your life."

The *why* is crucial because it will help you to understand your responses to various people and situations better. (Mike Shelah discussed finding your why in the previous chapter.) This is Michael's big lesson, and it's crucial to living the Mountaintop life. Understand yourself, get to know the *why* behind your choices and decisions, and focus more on your response to the world rather than on the stimulus.

I can apply Michael's powerful lessons to my own life, and I wish I had been exposed to him at an earlier age! When I was in high school, I had the passion and energy. What was lacking was my ability to take full ownership of my responses to other people. I would love to blame (sometimes consciously, sometimes without even thinking about it) society, my teachers, my friends, my parents, my teammates, and anyone else I could think of for areas of my life that were unhappy. But the truth is that I was the one fully responsible for my life.

To be clear, this does not mean I was responsible for the mean and hurtful actions of other people. I'm sure you can probably relate to encountering some real jerks from time to time. What Michael is saying here, and what I've learned over time, is that it's not about what someone else does to you, but how you respond that counts. You have more power over how you feel than you may have initially realized.

Thankfully, you can use these time-tested strategies to turn weird and dysfunctional situations to your advantage. Sometimes anxiety, confusion, and stress, which we all experience as human beings, shroud us from getting to know our true selves. Let these insights allow you to alleviate some of the pressure you put on yourself. Let's not derail ourselves, our success, and our impact by continuing to carry the weight of the world on our shoulders.

There are multiple paths to greatness. One path may not work, but there are many paths to your Mountaintop. Don't worry about other people judging you as weird. Focus more instead on your response to the situation and what you can do to move forward. Successful people put being true to themselves first.

As a freshman and sophomore at McDaniel College, I was continuing to go after my baseball dreams. I was on the college baseball team as a recruit athlete, but I didn't get any playing time. Already feeling a bit down, I heard of the opportunity to study abroad at McDaniel's main abroad campus in Budapest, Hungary. Most baseball players don't study abroad, but I jumped at the opportunity to make my college career more fun and exciting.

Here I am now, about a decade later, sharing with others how I found the hidden opportunity in my setback and how they can do the same. My college baseball experience, while painful at the time, was an awesome catalyst to this lifelong personal development practice to which I've dedicated myself. I was reluctant to go my own way because I genuinely wanted to please my coach. But when I finally realized that I was living my life to please a guy who wasn't going to give me playing time anyways, I mustered up the courage to study abroad for a whole year – which ended up being one of the best decisions of my life, giving me the enriching college experience I both wanted and deserved. And if I can find the silver lining in an unwanted situation, I'm certain you can as well.

People will try to limit you, consciously and unconsciously. Be respectful, but refuse to allow other people to dictate your life's direction or to make a decision for you.

I am honored that you've made it this far into the book, and you're reading these words. Please know you, the reader, truly are one of the special ones. In this book, I am using my own experiences as examples to help you. This journey that we are taking together through this book is about you and getting to your next level.

What we can all learn from Michael is that we can continuously evolve, become more patient with life, and stay grounded while exploring our purpose. With practice, we can learn not to let people get the best of us (like when they push our hot buttons, and we react reflexively, for example). This is all about being true to ourselves. Reaching our Mountaintop is about doing what's best for us instead of constantly seeking to please and to conform to other people's wishes and demands.

For example, to show I'm actively living the message of what I write, in order to finish this book in a reasonable amount of time, I left a lucrative consulting opportunity. Remember what I said earlier in this book about money being only one small factor of our success and oftentimes not the main factor? If I had most, if not all, of my focus on the consulting, then I would not have been able to bring my full self to this book. I want to make 100% sure that you have the best content possible in your hands to apply to your life and reach your Mountaintop. I don't want to be distracted by other people's agendas.

My biggest pet peeve is when people don't live their message, so I make sure that I'm following every little thing these experts are sharing with us, down to the tiniest detail. I'm definitely not perfect, and I often feel like I come up short, but I always do my best to apply these lessons in my own life.

Seeking to apply one kernel of insight in your life is one million times better than saying one thing and doing another. The smallest of actions is better than the biggest of false promises. Dreaming is wonderful and makes life tolerable, but you must follow-up on your dream with action. Do the work. Put in the time. Your future self will thank you.

What is also incredibly helpful and powerful from Michael's teachings is to favor quality over quantity. The depth of your impact matters more than the quantity of your impact. It's absolutely wonderful to reach many people at once, but remember that the quality of your impact is what counts the most.

Being a *real* person – someone of character and integrity – means caring deeply about individual needs and wants. Listen to others and genuinely help them without a hidden agenda. This is what leadership and true success are all about. It's emotional intelligence. That's reaching your Mountaintop.

More on Emotional Intelligence

"The second part of emotional intelligence," Michael said, "is relationship management and the ability to substitute knee-jerk reactions with even-tempered, well-reasoned, conscious choices. This is really the heart and soul of emotional intelligence. Being able to do this in the moment, when around other people, in practical application, is the key. Eighty percent of our behavior is based on our emotions, and yet most of us aren't in touch with our emotions. Spend time actually getting to know yourself and become aware of the kind of responses you want to create. This will then make it easier to recall those even-keeled responses in the moment, even when you feel those same old emotions of frustration and anger boiling to the surface."

Michael talked about the reflexive knee-jerk behavior that we've all been guilty of at some point in our lives. The vast majority of the time, we think about our behavior afterward and realize that we didn't represent our best selves.

"If you are in a truly dangerous situation," Michael said, "and you are in fight or flight mode, then fine, but if it is routine stress that is causing you to behave reactively, then that's not a good place to make decisions."

And most of the time, it's really routine stress that eats at us. Yes, there are absolutely going to be crises that arise, but if you dig a little more deeply, you will see the culprit to be the daily stress, not the one-off crazy situations.

For the record, as we discuss this, let me tell you that I am learning as much about this as you are. I have made *plenty* of mistakes in terms of blurting out things I didn't mean, saying things I later regretted, or doing things to hurt other people emotionally. I absolutely would never hurt anyone physically – I'm talking about emotional hurt. I'm an honest, loyal, and loving person, but when someone hurts me deeply my tendency is to want to say something that will hurt them back. What we're both learning from Michael is to be a better version of ourselves than we were in the past by learning and growing every day.

Recently, I was unexpectedly left hanging high and dry by two people who I thought to be good friends (these were two separate incidents not connected to each other). I easily could have said some hurtful insults to them, but I decided to be the bigger person and let it go. I can genuinely and sincerely say I applied Michael's teachings in my life. You no longer need to let other people get the best of you. You can find the silver lining, learn the lesson, and be the bigger person.

Michael's words on his personal development podcasts have helped me time and time again, and that's why I'm so incredibly excited to be sharing them here with you right now. Michael has a calm, centered presence that rubs off on others. It was an honor to meet him in La Crescenta-Montrose, California during one of his enlightening seminars.

I serve as a humble conduit between you and these successful leaders. It's my genuine and sincere intention to give you the knowledge, tools, information, and inspiration necessary to help you move to the next level in your life, whatever that next level may mean for you. Reaching your Mountaintop is about harnessing and refining your responses to life so that you are constantly growing towards that next level.

We are all equal. Yes, we all have different talents, abilities, and strengths, but our self-worth is infinite, and that makes us all equal. Please realize that you are equal to all of these experts here in this book. Before you know it, you'll be the one giving advice to others.

Finding the Right Mix in Your Life

"It all starts with your thoughts," Michael said. "The driver of your life is what you care about, and the results are seen in your behavior. If you go straight from emotions to behavior, it's like stepping on the gas with no steering wheel. If you have a thought and no emotion, then the car will be pointed in the right direction, but you will just sit there idling."

Michael laid out a solution for us to consider implementing in our own lives. The following is a mix of Michael's commentary and my own. The first sentence in each point is Michael, and the remaining explanation is my own.

- **Get pointed in the right direction.** This doesn't mean you have to be absolutely 100% crystal clear in every single area of your life, but you must, at the very least, have a general idea of where you're headed.
- **Care about what you're doing.** Believe in your life's purpose and establish habits to build around that purpose. Then persevere each day, which is the equivalent of channeling your emotions and pushing on the gas pedal to move forward. Don't let other people deter you or cause you to doubt yourself.

- **NOW you can begin moving forward with your achievements.** Literally, on this day, create time to work on your goals and dreams. If you are occupied today due to an obligation or prior commitment, then create time in the very near future to move forward and hold yourself to that commitment no matter what.

"The leaders are the women and men who figured this out," Michael said. "They figured out bad decisions and missed opportunities come from a stressed and scattered mind."

This is where the theme of this book comes into play yet again, as will often happen as we dive into the heart of each of these champions: working hard and moving forward with your goals while enjoying life at the same time is possible when you have not only the right mindset, authenticity, and leadership capabilities, but also a firm understanding of emotional intelligence. When you are moving forward with your goals on a daily basis, you will find it easier to handle the ups and downs of life because you are more centered. And when you are truly in the present moment, you will be able to manage your schedule better and focus on one thing at a time, which is what we were talking about earlier in terms of taking action and following through.

The beauty is that when the time comes to be with friends and family, you won't be distracted by what you should have done with your goals and purpose. How you do one thing is how you do everything, so when you become more emotionally intelligent and laser-focused on what you care about the most, other areas of your life (such as family life), will start to fall into place serendipitously. It won't happen all at once, and there will certainly be setbacks along the way, but it's definitely an achievable way of life with a little practice and persistence.

Awareness

"You can only help others if you first manage yourself," Michael said. "And you manage yourself by becoming aware. You can become aware of being aware. You can also become conscious of your consciousness. How do you find the elevated perspective? By taking a step back and rising above yourself. When you learn to do this, you then become more objective and more conscious. This is what higher consciousness and expanded awareness are all about.

"You can watch your thought processes and watch your feelings unfold with a higher level of understanding, realizing that certain feelings are just temporary storms," Michael emphasized.

You are a bright and intelligent individual, so let's go down the rabbit hole even further here:

"Awareness corresponds to spiritual love," Michael continued. "Awareness, or consciousness, is the spiritual love that transcends emotional turbulence. The soul is above and free of form with an elevated perspective. We can tap into the wisdom of our soul and communicate with it. That's where the intuition comes from. Then we become wiser than the full-blown thinking mind that drives us crazy. Full-blown ideas burst into awareness and arise with a 'That's it! That's the answer I was looking for!' These answers are all thought out and provided for us. That's the true self, above all of our frustrations."

Remember – the way to get in touch with this true self is to calm the emotions and still the mind. This is not always easy, but as we're learning from Michael, it's very possible. Reaching your Mountaintop is a process, a continual state of improvement, and it takes daily practice and discipline. There's no such thing as getting there. It's really about taking life one day, one step, at a time and learning along the way. The catch-22 here is that it's not a walk in the park, but it's easier than you might initially have thought, once you get going.

What this means in practical application is that if you sit around looking at a huge dream without doing anything, it's going to seem incredibly overwhelming. But if you get going and take steps forward, even if they are baby steps, you'll gain momentum and begin to conquer seemingly formidable obstacles.

"Don't think you have to have everything all figured out to get the process in motion," Michael said. "Most people think they have to have a still and calm mind to meditate, but they have it backward. You meditate to calm the mind. This is where we can then get in touch with our intuition."

"And reflection," I said, "reflection is key as well."

"Yes, well said," Michael affirmed. "The ability to reflect, to be aware that we are aware, is a special gift. Some would argue that's what it means to be made in the image of God. Roughly speaking, we've only had electric lights for 130 years; cars and planes for about 100 years; and we just got here as human beings, relative to the age of the universe. It seems that the essence of who we are is something we are just figuring out. The truth of who we are stands above our thoughts, feelings, and behavior. We can identify with that and be a higher level of awareness, and from there see the big picture."

The Illusion

"I joke with my friends that time is an illusion," I said to Michael. "It's an inside joke. But we mean it when we say it to one another, as we sincerely believe and know time is an illusion."

"Yes," Michael said. "And materialism is an illusion as well. We have to recognize that even if materialism is an illusion, it's a remarkable illusion. And even though we know time is an illusion, the Dalai Lama wears a Rolex® and carries a day planner."

This is absolutely not, in any way, shape, or form, taking away from the people who are immersed in time. In fact, it's doing just the opposite – it's establishing that we all live in time and must deal with it on a practical basis. Michael is not telling you to ditch your day planner; rather, he is suggesting to maintain your day planner and daily to-dos within a higher level of conscious awareness. It is from this elevated perspective that we make better choices, have less stress, and stay true to the center of who we are. This is what will help to ensure that you are reaching YOUR Mountaintop, your version of success.

Don't think that this has to be complicated. Yes, it takes time, yes it requires patience, but it all starts with one moment: this moment. Observe your breath. Become more conscious. Wake yourself up.

"There are people who have been meditating their entire lives and yet they still continue to practice it each day," Michael said. "Watch your breath the same way you'd watch the waves roll in and out."

This is not a one-off, quick-fix tip – it's a habit and daily discipline you will grow with time. If meditation works for you, great. And if there is something else you do that gets you in touch with yourself, that's great too. The point here is not to get rigorously attached to some dogma or way of doing things; it's to get in touch with yourself by finding your own truth and doing what works for you. Once you are fully in touch with yourself, you will be able to manage yourself better within this illusion called life.

"It's a paradox," Michael said. "No two fingerprints are alike, yet diversity stems from unity. We must get comfortable with the relative nature of life. God is absolute, but life is relative."

The Hidden Gift

"You are always connected to God," Michael said. "Even when it doesn't feel like it. Think of thoughts as being submitted to your awareness for your approval. What you do with those thoughts is up to you. If you want to accept them, reject them, or replace them, it's your choice."

Once again, Michael's wisdom is profound. I've often heard it said that you are responsible for every one of your thoughts. I disagree; you are not necessarily responsible for every single thought that comes to your awareness, as random thoughts pop up all the time, but you are responsible for *what you do* with those thoughts. That's why Michael's words of wisdom make sense.

Fear often causes us to lose sight of that connection we all have with one another. Here is Michael's take on fear:

"Fear," Michael said, "is a feeling or set of feelings we don't understand about a situation or ourselves, dangerous or not. If you are still afraid and just don't know why, it is fear you don't understand or know about yourself or your situation. But all fear is fear of the unknown; it's the brain's appeal for a better understanding. The antidote to fear is self-awareness; you can learn to be more aware, bring your attention into the present moment, and train yourself to become conscious of the temptation to be distracted by the past or the future. Continually bring yourself back to the present moment and you will better understand and work through fear.

"This awareness is what allows you to stay connected; it's the antidote to all forms of fear: worry, doubt, apprehension, etc. All negative feelings, everything that hurts, irritates, or frustrates us, are forms of fear. Fear is not just one negative feeling. It includes all the different variations of negative feelings and emotions that arise. Look underneath the hood! If your heart hurts, it's an indication of something deeper you don't understand about yourself. Understand yourself better and the heartache goes away. If the negative feeling persists it means there are more presents underneath the tree; you didn't get all of your gifts. So repeat the process and look at the feeling again," Michael explained.

What Michael said here is so incredibly powerful that it's worth repeating and emphasizing: *if the negative feeling persists it means there are more presents underneath the tree.* This is a profound and remarkable insight, and not one to discard easily. What this means is underneath all of the negativity, anger, and frustration is a peaceful state of understanding and awareness. Anything that causes you grief can lead to more wisdom and understanding when you bring it into the light of your conscious awareness.

I was recently in Europe for vacation, and in the middle of a beautiful, sunny, warm day, I suddenly found myself angry and upset with the baseball situations of my past. At first, I started to judge myself for thinking about this because I thought it was something I was completely over, but then I remembered Michael's words and realized it was an opportunity to better understand both the situation and myself at a deeper level. Instead of resisting the feeling, I consciously breathed in and out. I also shared my feelings with someone close to me to help release the negativity. The strategies worked, and I ended up realizing that the less-than-kind actions of my teammates had nothing to do with me – it was about *their* personality and character. The peace that ensued came because I faced the feelings directly.

Before we leave this section, let's let Michael drive the point home:

"The power, the incredible insight in our negative feelings," he said, "is that enfolded within them is a gift. Negative feelings are your higher self's way of getting your attention and teaching you more about yourself and the situation you may find yourself in. Sit quietly in an expanded state of awareness, look at the feeling, and it will expose itself to you. When you get the full understanding, the hurt will go away. I emphasize that if the negative feeling persists, it means there is a part of you that is carrying and holding onto it."

You Have Options

One of the best lessons I learned from Michael through years of listening to his radio shows and podcasts is that you have options. Most of the time, you have more options than you may have initially realized.

The solution to your challenge may not necessarily be cut and dry. It may be a different permutation and combination of solutions than you were initially thinking. Remembering that you have options, and becoming aware of different choices you can make increases your level of freedom. It is a normal emotion to feel like you are trapped in your current situation. Michael is saying when you really sit down to analyze the possibilities and opportunities, more options will come to you. A big theme of this book and Mountaintop-level life is knowing you always have a choice.

You may not end up going with plan A, B, or C. Instead, you may go with plan X, Y, or Z. Gregg Chase, a screenwriter, creative director, designer, and former coworker of mine, supports our discussion. Like Michael, Gregg knows the power of going with additional options. I mention Gregg here because he referenced Plan Z to me in the past and I thought it was a brilliant concept.

Step Away From It All and Reduce Your Stress

Before we wrap up this chapter with some parting shots from Michael, I'm going to add in some excellent insight from Christine Southworth, a speaker and stress reduction expert. Her tips are about really taking control of your emotions and remaining even-keeled.

"Multi-tasking leads *directly* to stress," Christine emphasized.

I laughed because I was multi-tasking the entire morning before we spoke.

"Yes, I multi-task more often that I'd like to admit," I said.

"Don't feel bad," Christine said. "Multi-tasking is the norm for most. People feel guilty if they're not connected to technology 24/7. But the key to stress reduction is to step away from that stuff. People don't take the time to be alone and to be mindful, and that's why their minds are running at increasingly dizzying speeds."

"Very well put," I said, "and similar to what some of the other experts I've talked with said. It's no wonder you are successful. Speaking of which, what are some strategies one can apply to reach their Mountaintop, their own version of success, without feeling so overwhelmed?"

"It's medically proven that mindfulness and meditation for ten minutes a day restructures the brain and makes you less reactive," Christine said. "And equally importantly, it makes you less receptive to stress."

"That's a great reminder," I said, "because my friend, Michael Benner, was saying the exact same thing. I've been applying it, but not as much as I need to."

"I understand that," Christine said. "It's hard to find the time, and it's normal to have a lot going on. Just gently guide yourself back to finding ten minutes a day to meditate, or even for taking deep, conscious breaths. It will significantly improve your health in more ways than one.

"Meditating is scary to some people, but really it's just breathing. Just *breathe*. You can do it with a cup of coffee. Use your senses."

This simple yet *incredibly* powerful strategy from Christine will increase your personal effectiveness while making you happier, healthier, and more aware. She and Michael are both outstanding emotional intelligence experts! Let us always remember that intelligently managing our emotions is vital each day of our lives.

Partings Shots

"Where do you get your youthful enthusiasm and passion for life?" I asked Michael.

"Consciousness doesn't age," Michael said. "I may be in my sixties, but I still feel like I did when I was twenty."

"Any parting words of wisdom?" I asked.

"Yes," Michael said. "Visualization for attaining goals is helpful. And speaking of goals, if you find yourself getting bored with your goals or life, just think of it as another distracted thought. Bored is nothing more than a decision to quit. Don't have unrealistic expectations about other people. Rather, turn the attention; focus within on how you can better yourself, become more conscious, and practice even-keeled responses."

Michael's words are so powerful; a big problem in my younger years is that I expected too much from people and thus was constantly let down. But when I traveled through Europe I learned to go with the flow of each moment and see where it took me. I learned when you are centered within yourself, happiness and peace will find you. But when you are constantly searching for the answers, the potential for freedom and liberation will elude you.

This book is about reaching your Mountaintop. And within reaching your Mountaintop, the key kernel is to become more conscious. Becoming conscious is really about focusing on what's in your control. You can't control other people, but you can control yourself. This is the beauty of the reach-your-Mountaintop process – you no longer have to be dependent on the whims and fancies of others. You can stay calm, centered, and focused, ready to do the improbable.

"Thank God Michael Jordan didn't quit after just three attempts," Michael said. "A lot of people give up on improving their awareness because they find it too difficult. People are so familiar with their fear, stress, and anxiety that they really don't want to give it up. Many people would rather have fear and suffering that is familiar than the understanding and peace that is new and different.

"My biggest encouragement is to become more mindful and aware in each moment of life. Notice that most people's small talk is a never-ending appeal for sympathy. Without the suffering, people would have nothing to talk about. Gossip, which is talking about other people, should be avoided at all costs. Eleanor Roosevelt explained to the world how great minds talk about ideas; mediocre minds talk about events; and small minds talk about other people. Train yourself to talk about ideas rather than other people.

"Sadly, most adult conversation has degenerated into gossip. People are making a choice to do that. No one is doing it to them; rather, their choice to gossip is their response to the world. Change your response and watch your whole day, week, month, and year unfold differently.

"Finally, you *must* really look at what is bothering you," Michael continued. "You must really, truly face it. No pretending and no faking. You must really face that pain and suffering. If you allow yourself truly to feel it and face it, you will find yourself finally being open to getting past it. You die to the pain and thus transcend the pain. The real pain is in the resistance. The more you resist, the tighter you grab the pain and suffering. But there is wisdom in letting your thoughts and feelings just be as they are, observing them from a detached perspective. Instead of worrying about letting go, just focus on your breath and breathe into the moment. Breathe into that tension. Doesn't it feel good?"

"Michael – I'm speechless. Your wisdom is legendary, to say the least," I said.

I love how Michael's lessons strike that balance between being focused and working on goals while being truly in the present moment and liberating yourself. In a practical and legitimate way, you can enjoy the journey on the way to your goal and your Mountaintop.

"Don't think that you will be happy someday. Happiness *is* the way to your goal. Most people think that achieving a goal is the way to becoming happy, but the truth is becoming happy is the way to achieving a goal," Michael said.

Once again, Michael's words ring true. Instead of carrying the entire world on your shoulders, seek to be calm and happy in the present moment. Achieve this and you will no longer live each day feeling overwhelmed.

"If it gets really bad for you at times, then take life one breath at a time," Michael said. "Break it down moment by moment. That's where you will find your freedom."

And that, my friends, is the epitome of emotional intelligence when it comes to moving forward with your goals while enjoying and revolutionizing life – reaching your Mountaintop without stressing or feeling burned out.

Emotional Intelligence is Essential

There you have it: Michael and Christine emphasized how incredibly important it is to take control of your responses, harness your emotions, become aware, establish a stress reduction process (like meditation and mindfulness), and give yourself time to breathe.

Reaching your Mountaintop is not about doing everything at once. Yes, you need a general sense of urgency in knowing that your time here on the planet is short, but maintain a sense of calmness. Being in control of your emotions is the cornerstone of a Mountaintop-level way of life. Just because someone has treated you unfairly does not mean you need to stoop to their level. Be the bigger person.

P.S. Check out Michael's new book, *Fearless Intelligence*, coming soon

Questions for Reflection

1.   What are your hot buttons and pet peeves? How can you stay more in control when someone does something to you which you don't like?

2.   What are some ways that work for you to increase your level of awareness and consciousness? Talking to a friend? Going on a walk? Watching an inspiring movie? Something else?

3.   What time of the day works best for you to take ten to fifteen minutes (or whatever amount of time works best for you) of personal reflection, solitude, and/or meditation time?

Chapter 6: Become the Expert

"I can't help but think, had I been introduced to this material when I was younger, I would have gotten to where I wanted to be about twenty years sooner, with far fewer mistakes."
– Mike Shelah

You might be thinking right now, *Ok, Jeff – pretty good job so far, you made some well-thought-out points through the people you've featured. I see some of the skills I need to master in order to slowly, but surely, move beyond those nagging doubts, and I certainly know the importance of staying true to myself and becoming more aware. But, when it comes to achieving more and making an impact, half the time I don't know what to focus on, and the other half I'm not focusing at all!*

My friend: I know that feeling all too well. No exaggeration, years of my life have been stuck in indecision. And then when I finally made a decision, I would question myself even further and feel like I made the wrong choice! It's as if the doubt never ends. But you can apply a specific, actionable process that will lead you to take massive action.

Yesterday I was chatting with a couple of friends over lunch at a restaurant/bar in Westerly, Rhode Island, and they asked me how I was able to distribute my first book through a publisher internationally, across three different continents, while going to graduate school at Johns Hopkins, working for the Government, growing my business, expanding my reach, traveling, and constantly networking. The answer was that while it seemed like I had a million things going on, my *one thing* was publishing my book. Everything funneled into that. Establishing myself as an expert in my field by becoming an author is what led me to become an entrepreneur.

They smiled, and I explained that while I have enormous amounts of energy, I have a knack for seeing ideas through to completion. When I get new ideas, I jot them down in Evernote. However, I've always stayed with one idea at a time. Trying new things is definitely a good thing, but in a world where everyone is so quick to quit and stop a project halfway, my consistency and self-discipline have served me well.

You can be the most talented person in the world, but all the gift and ability in the world means nothing if you don't put in the hard work, effort, and consistency required to focus and reach your Mountaintop.

There are no shortcuts here. But, on a good note, these are insights you will definitely be able to put into action for yourself. Let's now hear from more experts about how to really hone in on an area of expertise as you climb your Mountain and head towards epic success.

Meeting Randy Gage

Growing my speaking career, I decided to go to the National Speakers Association annual conference in Washington, D.C., in July of 2015. It was a wonderful opportunity, and I learned a lot of tips about how to take my business to the next level. I'm extremely independent, and I don't like to follow set rules, but I've found that there's value in being on someone else's schedule at times. The National Speakers Association is a very credible, legitimate, and useful organization, so the four-day conference was well worth my time.

On the final day of the conference, successful singer, humorist, and speaker Jane Herlong was sitting next to me at lunch. She liked my energy and said,

"You know, Jeff, if you're really serious about growing your speaking business, you should go and talk to Randy Gage."

She pointed diagonally, and there sitting at a table near us was Randy Gage. The table was full.

"I'd go up to him right now," she said. "Tell him you'd like to learn about his success. Just make sure that you do more listening than talking. Randy really knows how to add value to his clients. His insights are very useful."

I had a few more bites of my meal and then I went over to the table he was sitting at.

"Hey Randy, I'm Jeff Davis," I said. "Would love to sit down with you and chat for a few minutes and ask you a few questions about your success and how you got to where you are."

Randy smiled.

"Would love to, but not this instant," Randy said. "Catch me right after lunch is over and I'd be happy to chat with you."

Randy is an author, professional speaker, entrepreneur, and marketer with an amazing story of overcoming some incredibly challenging setbacks, such as dropping out of school, being in a jail cell as a teen, getting shot in the abdomen, and nearly becoming bankrupt. His book, *Risky is The New Safe*, became a bestseller, as have his other books. He's spoken in more than fifty countries and has inspired millions of people around the world, making millions in the process. He lives his message and is incredibly authentic – a perfect match for this book.

With lunch still going, I ran into some women from my home state of Connecticut. They didn't know I was in DC and excitedly asked me a bunch of questions, impressed I was able to make it to the "mother ship" (the national conference is where all the individual local chapters of the National Speakers Association across the United States and the world come together).

As often happens in conversations, time slipped by and when I looked around I couldn't find Randy. But there's enormous value in seeing someone face-to-face, even if only briefly, because when I contacted Randy afterward he was kind enough to continue the conversation with me over the phone.

Find Your Area of Expertise and Become the Thought Leader

Randy and I got right into it and talked about the challenges of growing a business.

"You can grow your business by cold calling, but I'd rather poke my eyes out than make cold calls," Randy said. "The key is to become the go-to expert on a given subject."

"What is it for you?" I asked.

"Prosperity," Randy said.

Randy is talking about something called inbound marketing, where you put out lots of expert content into the world and have people see and think of you as the expert in a given field.

"When I started growing my speaking business I didn't have the Internet like you do, so I used to publish articles in magazines and put my 800 number at the end of it," Randy said. "With the ease of the Internet, you can more easily put stuff out there."

"Easier said than done," I replied with a light laugh. "But I've come to think of it as a process to embrace."

"You're right," Randy said. "Ask yourself: what are you an expert in? Look at your experiences, what other people tell you that you're good at, and what you feel is your calling. Then put out massive amounts of content via your website to show that you're the authority."

If you're starting completely from scratch, you can still choose to cold call, but when it comes to becoming an authority you definitely want to focus on creating content and pushing it out to the world as an expert. You can discuss other topics if you want to, but make sure you have that number one focus – that one thing you're known for.

Ask yourself: what is the one topic you want to become the expert in the most? Pick one area of expertise and put your whole heart and soul into it. You are going to have a tendency to want to jump into a lot of different topics but start with your favorite initiative, the topic that jacks you up so much that you can't wait to tell the world about what you're doing. That's where you will become the expert.

Focusing on one topic does not mean you are limited to one kind of activity, as there are a lot of mediums and methods to spread your message: blogging, YouTube, social media channels, and other kinds of forums. It just means your thoughts, words, actions, and overall initiatives are all in alignment. I'd also suggest developing the skill of single-handling, where you focus on not only one topic at a time, but one activity at a time.

Reaching your Mountaintop is about focusing in on the areas and topics you care about the most. For me, it's suicide prevention and helping people get through tough

times by finding the hidden opportunity in their setback
(story behind why I'm so passionate about this is in the
beginning of the book): a lot of my content is geared
around helping others to get through dark times, helping
others to get through their own storms, and providing
others with ways to connect with their specific purpose. I
speak to people of all ages and backgrounds, but my main
niche is youth: specifically, high school and college
students. This also includes speaking at associations,
conferences, and nonprofit organizations involving these
topics.

If you don't know what topic to become the authority
in, start where you are. What do you know a lot about? Or,
what do you care about so much that you would love to
study and learn about it as much as you possibly can?
What societal problems bother you the most? Where do
you feel you could have the most impact in society? Take a
few minutes to really think about this – it's never too early
or late to engage in this process. Go into meditation about
it if you're not getting an answer right away. What lights
you on fire? What problems do you feel people aren't doing
enough about? That could be a potential opportunity where
you could achieve a unique and meaningful impact. As you
continue putting out insightful content in your area of
choice, you will eventually be known as a thought leader.

"Randy, what you're saying is spot on," I said. "Just
playing Devil's advocate, though, I read *Money Talks*, by
Alan Weiss, and he says NOT to limit yourself to a specific
niche or industry. What are your thoughts on that?"

"I know Alan, and he's a smart guy," Randy said. "Still
have your area of expertise, but be aware that it applies to
all different kinds of industries. For example, being an

expert in leadership can apply to the banking industry, corporations, nonprofits, sports teams, and other industries. This is why it's so important to become a thought leader, gaining visibility across multiple industries on a given subject matter."

In my case (I'm using this as an example as you think about this for yourself) getting through dark times can apply to different industries other than students. For example, studies show a huge percentage of the workforce is stressed and burnt out – my knowledge applies to their situation. I also speak to nonprofits about improving morale and implementing more purpose and meaning into their daily actions. So just because you have one area of expertise does not mean you are limiting yourself.

"In terms of becoming a thought leader," Randy said, "it's about having the confidence to literally lead thought."

Haters Are Going to Hate, But Don't Let It Get to You

"What about people who criticize and condemn us?" I asked Randy.

"We all have haters," Randy said. "But as you develop true self-confidence, it's a matter of pushing past the haters and putting your best stuff out there to the world. That's what will cause you to really make a difference.

"I spoke at the million-dollar roundtable at the National Speakers Association conference in Washington, D.C. – these were all speakers who were making an income in the millions. I gave them the top ten essentials of truly being a thought leader, and one of them was having haters," Randy said.

It is what it is. Having haters is a simple byproduct of having expanded reach and influence. It's not a pleasant experience, and I wish it weren't the case, but it is one thing to watch out for as you really zero in on becoming a thought leader in your area. I want everyone to like me, but what I've realized is that this won't always happen. Do your best and be true to yourself; if some people aren't ok with that, forget about them and switch your focus back to your purpose and power. As Randy says, "in order to become a thought leader and make a difference, you must give up the need to be liked."

Don't change for every critic. Disregard the naysayers. Realize that their errant opinions don't affect your destiny. I'm a sensitive guy, and I struggle with this, but I'm getting better at it every day. And so can you.

This is why the chapters leading up to this one have provided us with such a strong foundation. The soft skills ARE the hard skills: overcoming doubt, mastering your mindset, being authentic, being emotionally intelligent, becoming a leader, trusting yourself, and everything else we covered so far. These are the key characteristics of someone who has the maturity and wherewithal to not be pulled in a million different directions, but rather choose to increase their impact by focusing on one thing at a time.

It takes genuine and authentic levels of courage and confidence to push past the haters when you are focusing on the one area of expertise you are mastering. Don't let the critics and insulters throw you off your game. Shrug them off and push forward even harder. Randy Gage is the man. Take his advice on this subject and watch your influence expand as you head for the Mountaintop.

One Thing

My discussion with Dave Wheeler, a speaker coach, consultant, and business owner, was also very valuable. I met Dave through Toastmasters, a powerful organization that helps to develop your public speaking and leadership skills, and his insights are the perfect addition to what we've already been discussing here.

After a successful career in engineering and manufacturing, in 2009 Dave embraced the entrepreneurial mindset.

"What makes all the difference is focusing on that one thing," Dave said. "Ask yourself: what one thing will make the completion of all my other tasks easier? Don't worry about micromanaging every segment of every hour of every day. Instead, worry about how your activities are molding to fit the one thing. Until your one thing is done, everything else is a distraction."

"I hear you completely, Dave," I said, "and I agree. But there are many people out there with multiple projects going on, and they don't know which one to choose as their number one focus. What are your thoughts on that?"

"There is such a thing as a halo effect," Dave said. "When you get really focused on one thing, a lot of the junk gets thrown away. And those number two and number three projects get pulled along. For example, I work with speakers and consultants on increasing their value. Once they land that big paycheck, a lot of their other initiatives fall into place more easily."

"The lightbulb just went on, Dave," I said with a smile. "As someone who likes to understand why people do things, this makes sense. How you do one thing is how you do everything. For me, right now, it's this book. I've been working on it for several years, but I know with added focus, I can finish it in the near future. Once I get this book out there and go on my book tour, the benefits for my business will be huge. And most importantly of all, I'm focused on the benefit this book will have to society and how it will help individual people get through challenges on their way to their Mountaintop, their own version of success."

"You got it," Dave said with a smile. "Sounds like you have a good plan and have found your one thing."

Dave is packed with all sorts of wisdom and insight; he's great.

"What about balance and reducing stress?" I asked. "Doesn't that get thrown out the window when you are only focusing on one thing? For example, I'm more than halfway done with writing this book, and I've been sleeping less as I sacrifice to get this done."

"Try and get the right amount of sleep, as studies show that enhances your productivity," Dave said. "But balance is overrated. Setting really good goals and chasing them is the way to go. A lot of people would think that's work, but if you have something you like and care about, it becomes fun. And keep in mind this doesn't have to just be a goal in the classic sense. It could be a relationship or person you're passionate about as well. There are all sorts of fringe benefits to temporarily unbalancing your life in the short-term, because it will make things a heck of a lot easier in the long-run."

Dave is a very smart man and has helped, mentored, and coached lots of people. Wouldn't you agree that it makes sense to take his advice and run with it?

Narrow it Down

The third expert on this subject I'd like to introduce to you is Michael Lynch, a speaker, blogger, and coach who is focused on helping millennials become successful entrepreneurs. With a background in sales and marketing, Michael has a lot of great insights to share.

I first met Michael at one of the entrepreneurial networking groups I regularly attend. My speaker friend, Bill Corbett, suggested I introduce myself to Michael, so I did. A few weeks later we decided to meet at Archie Moore's Bar and Restaurant in Wallingford, Connecticut, and had a productive conversation.

"The danger is that if you start too broad, you'll never end up picking that one thing and running with it," Michael said.

"What about many of my speaker friends who speak on all sorts of different topics?" I asked.

"I'd have to imagine at one point in time they picked one thing and ran with it," Michael said. "And then from there, branched out."

We talked about one another's business, and different things we have going on. Ambition is a fantastic trait to have, but it can become dangerous when you are wanting to take on too much at once.

"If you are constantly looking around, seeing what others are doing, and feeling that you can do it all, there might come a time when you realize you never put a post in the ground and established some expertise," Michael said. "At some point, you just have to pick something and run with it.

"You have critics. I have critics. We all have critics," Michael said. "But when you focus on that one thing, it allows you to more easily make an impact while blocking out distractions."

By all means, have multiple projects going on. Build your empire. Break the rules. Do what your intuition tells you to do. And don't be afraid to say "yes" to something. Just please make sure there comes a time when you do what Randy, Dave, and Michael are saying to do: pick that one thing and run with it.

Even With Lots of Plates Spinning, Focus on One Thing at a Time

Remember that reaching your Mountaintop means doing what works for you. I'm going to offer author Nick Thacker's input here as interesting additional input to what we just heard from the above three champions, because one of the goals of this book is to get you to look at things from different angles, question everything, and find the right mix that works for you.

The following input does not, in any way, detract from what we just heard. Rather, it adds in some additional thoughts from someone who is sharing what works for him:

"I sometimes wish I could devote my entire pool of energy to just one thing, but I don't think I was wired that way," Nick said. "I usually have a thousand proverbial plates spinning and I like it that way.

"I wouldn't advise that people only focus on one thing. However, knowing what type of person you are can change that answer. If you love having a very structured, set system every day, then focusing on one passion until you see it through can be a great strategy.

"Still, I don't think passions are the same as projects. A passion for me, for example, is writing. So while I might focus on five different projects during a week, they all might be within that one passion. I do believe there's power in seeing things through. Quitting isn't always a bad thing, but I believe it takes practice to learn our own 'quitting parameters'. If you've never tried writing a book, you're probably going to want to quit.

"But most writers I know (myself included) want to quit at least once during the process – even after we've written ten books. So if it's your first book, you'd probably be wise to commit to it and see it through, and then learn more about yourself and when it's right or not right for you to quit. Then, after you've made it through the process, you'll have a much better understanding of whether or not writing books is your thing.

"The challenge we all face is in designing life to be a perfect balance of things we're passionate about, that we have the freedom to become experts in, without needing to worry about money," Nick continued. "Many people assume that means their passion should become their job and vice versa, but that isn't the best combination for everyone.

"Realize that your passion and your job aren't always the same thing, but it's a mistake to think you should quit the passion side of things because it doesn't make as much as your job. It's also a mistake, often, to think you should quit the job because it's not providing you the passion you desire/deserve," Nick emphasized.

To add to Nick's input here, you can absolutely switch to a new job or career if your current situation is making you completely miserable (something I've done several times). Nick is saying that it's good to have steady income while you grow your passion and become a big enough expert in it to someday make substantial money from it.

"The answer to this equation, Jeff," Nick said, "is different for everyone. Figure out what the balance is for you and then put up with the consequences. If you can't put up with it, change the equation or change the solution. It takes time and it's not always easy."

Notice that Nick is not dictating a certain way of living, acting, or doing. He is merely suggesting for you to find what works for you. While his thoughts do offer a bit of juxtaposition to the commentary earlier in this chapter, he also is in agreement in the sense that even when he has a lot going on he can only really focus on one thing at a time. While he has a lot going at the same time, he still becomes the expert by have a general grouping for his projects.

What works for you? What is your balance point? Do what makes sense for your current situation. I emphasize this because I always get annoyed when I read books where the author says their conclusion is the set way of doing something. Their input may be great, but it doesn't always apply to my situation. Pull into your life what you feel is most beneficial.

Understand and Apply These Seven Principles and Reap a Lifetime of Achievement

Let's synthesize the amazing expertise we've come across in this chapter. In closing, I'd like to leave you with seven main points as you start with one thing:

1. Get to know yourself better by reflecting and meditating. What are you good at? What's an area

where you have a lot of interest? Don't be afraid to follow your passion, even if someone told you not to do it. This is YOUR choice, not someone else's.

2.   Embrace self-doubt. Think of doubt as a signpost telling you which direction to choose. We all have multiple things we are good at. Just start with one thing and work your way forward from there. Even see if there is a way to combine multiple passions into one activity (for example, someone who likes traveling and writing could become a travel writer). Worst case scenario, you try something and it turns out to not be a subject you want to be an expert in. No big deal: now you have further insight into your psyche, and you can decide to switch to something else that is more to your liking.

3.   Question the negativity. At one point or another, everyone growing a business runs into struggles. Don't let those negative thoughts take you over. Look at the evidence. Your doubts are traitors, and oftentimes not the truth. Our minds have a way of looking at the worst possible outcomes instead of focusing on the silver lining. Looking at the facts helps you to see that a lot of your negativity does not have basis in reality. This is the truth, even if you can't see it while the doubts are swirling around in your head.

4.   Give yourself a pep talk. Believe it or not, successful people talk to themselves. Remind yourself of your great qualities. Make a list of five things you've achieved that you're really proud of. When you are nervous or anxious about

something coming up, remind yourself of your successes and wins from the past. Get your mind off of the possibility of something bad happening. Instead, recall peak performances and moments of happiness from your past.

5. Building off of point number four, take the time to visualize your desired outcome. Visualize yourself as a person who is strong, confident, and decisive. Imagine the feelings of pride, happiness, and personal accomplishment you'll have once you focus your efforts on a single goal and finish it to completion. Affirm your future reality as if it has already occurred in the present moment. I used to think visualization was not worth my time, but when situations in real life started to unfold as I visualized them I connected the link to the power of this practice. Please know visualization doesn't guarantee an outcome, but it does increase the likelihood of it happening.

6. Remember that everyone who is now a big-time expert was once a beginner. Have fun with the process. Make time for solitude in your daily schedule. Trust yourself. Yes, the point of this chapter is to get you to become an expert in something you care about, but remember that you are in complete control of your life. And no matter what anyone else thinks, says, or does, you are always free to change direction if that's what you feel is in your best interest. Just make sure you are changing direction so that you can focus on one thing, and not bouncing around from one thing to the next.

7. Make a decision. I know, as well as anyone on this planet, how hard this one can be. I know what it's like to be caught in indecision. To this day, I wonder if I would have been better off positioning myself as a budget travel expert instead of a youth behavior expert, given my massive and extensive travels across the world. But helping youth is my ultimate purpose and passion, so that's my focus. And I still travel all the time on weekends and holidays, so it's not like I've stopped traveling. I share this to help you with your own process.

Onwards and Upwards

If you've made it this far in this book, you are in the elite few. I mean that from the bottom of my heart. Most people don't make it this far in the books they buy. Now, more than halfway through the book, you're going to love who we hear from next.

Questions for Reflection

1. What one thing do you want to do the most? What one thing lights you on fire? What problem in society do you feel you could help with the most?
2. What is a topic or body of knowledge you've been wanting to master? What are some of the best books in this field you could buy, or borrow from the local library, in the near future?
3. What are ways you could take action to test your ideas, achieve better clarity, and come to a decision?

Chapter 7: Manage Time at the Mountaintop and Find Your Balance

"Being busy is a form of laziness –
lazy thinking and indiscriminate action."
– Tim Ferriss

You're committed to developing expertise in a given field, or at least you're starting to think about some topics you'd love to be known for. Now you must get really good at managing your time. This is a core skill as you climb your Mountain and often means the difference between success and failure. In today's digital age of never-ending distraction, it is critical to become good at scheduling and managing your time. Think of your ability to manage time as the fulcrum by which you move yourself to ascend your Mountain.

Time management isn't something to just think about and discard. It affects every aspect of your life because time management is really life management. It is critical that leaders know how to manage their time effectively. In order to climb and reach your Mountaintop, you must be conscious of how you spend most of your time. What are your habits? What are your daily actions?

Let's hear from more geniuses and experts on what they have to say about time management.

Schedule Everything

In early March of 2015, I was at a marketing conference in San Diego (the one I told Ann Meacham I was going to). I posted a picture on Facebook of me in the city, and my friend Lindsay Siegel saw it and commented that I should reach out to John Lee Dumas.

I didn't reach out to John asking to be on his podcast – I just wanted to say hello. It's a great example of good things happening when you don't have a hidden agenda, because although we didn't get to meet in person, he asked me to be on his podcast anyway!

His *Entrepreneur on Fire* podcast is one of the top in the world, and the exposure was simply incredible. Before we did the podcast, I asked him if I could mention him in this book, and he said absolutely. As we spoke on the phone, I asked him some important questions.

There are three stand-out tips from my conversation with him that I want to share with you. They are incredibly powerful and, when properly applied, will improve your results:

1. Schedule everything.
2. Take breaks.
3. Surround yourself with the right people.

"If it's not on the calendar, it probably won't happen," John said to me as we chatted on the phone.

"What about simple things like meditation?" I asked with a smile.

"Put that on the calendar too – put it all on the calendar. What I've found is that when you don't schedule time for the things you want to get done, your other activities will find a way to push that activity out, often without you even realizing it. Make sure that even the little activities you care about are scheduled," John emphasized.

This is awesome input because it ties into a core theme of this chapter: make time for the things YOU want to do. Yes, there are always going to be chores, obligations, and other tasks that you have to do as part of being a human being on planet Earth, but you have more control over your schedule than you may realize.

Believe it or not, you can schedule into your calendar some fun and tension-relieving activities like going for a massage, spending time with family, working out, watching a movie, and activities like those. The whole point of managing your time well is to leave time for the fun things and get time to relax! Sounds simple and obvious, but many people get caught up in the mode of "go, go, go" (I've been as guilty of this as anyone) and forget that being productive isn't supposed to leave you feeling burned out – it's supposed to leave you feeling fulfilled so you can do the things you actually want to do.

It's fantastic to be in the flow and getting lots of things done – I love that feeling, don't you?

The second aspect of John's insightful comments to discuss is taking breaks. Research shows that when you take a 5-minute break every hour, your productivity increases. So don't feel like you have to do everything at once. Be focused, but make sure to pace yourself and give yourself breaks along the way.

"What do you do when you get overwhelmed or stressed?" I asked John.

"Walks, for me, are huge," John said. "They help me keep my sanity, maintain peace, find my balance, get answers, and remember to keep it all in perspective. Walks are a huge part of my daily schedule, and I make sure to make time for them."

This is very powerful because John is a living example of strong time management leading to more peace, not more stress. He makes sure to take care of himself and take breaks along the way, and it has led him to massive success.

His third tip is an important reminder to always be careful who you surround yourself with. As you read this book, and specifically this chapter, you are saturating yourself with positive insights, which is good, but you need to be aware of the people in your life. It can be challenging to find new friends, though, so don't beat yourself up when it takes longer than you want it to take. Just please be careful who you are spending your time with on a daily, weekly, monthly, and yearly basis. It makes a huge difference in your life.

You've heard this tip earlier in the book, but it's worth repeating because it's so incredibly important to your success. If you apply everything from these chapters but are around the wrong people, you will quickly lose steam.

"You are the average of the five people you spend the most time with," John said.

Get around people who are doing what you want to do. Ask them questions. Reach out and initiate meetings. Do what you have to do to get all sorts of great input from successful people.

Five Practical Tips to Get More Done in Less Time

The goal of managing your time well is to be able to have fun and spend time doing things you enjoy. The result of effectively managing time is to get rid of the feeling of being continually bogged down, stressed, and overwhelmed. We all know that feeling too well.

Have you ever struggled to start, continue, or finish a looming project? I know I have, and I know the feeling of being incomplete because of it. Here are five tips to reinvent the way you approach time management that will have you feeling better and more fulfilled than you did before:

Start Small

When faced with a ridiculously large task or project, don't think of all the work you have to do. Instead, think in fifteen-minute segments. If fifteen minutes seems like too much given your fast-paced, demanding, and hectic day-to-day life, try working on it for five minutes or even two or three minutes at a time.

You're probably wondering what good will the small dent of five minutes of work do for a large project. Several things. First, there is such a thing as a momentum principle where five minutes can easily turn into ten minutes, and ten into twenty, etc. Second, even if you only have five to ten minutes total to work on a given task in a day, some work is always better than no work. For example, I'm working on another book right now (this book you are presently reading) and at the end of a long, busy day, when I work on my book for a few minutes before going to sleep I always feel ten times better than if I didn't work on it at all. I may only have written one page, but that's one more page of the book that's complete. And for the evenings when I'm simply too tired to work on the book, I make it a point to wake up a little earlier than usual to continue making progress toward the goal.

Third, where the evolution of time management comes in, it's about how you feel rather than what you get done. If you work on something for five minutes, feel happy, and know you are making progress, who cares if you are done with it yet or not! Of course, the goal is to get it done as productively and effectively as possible, but you don't have to put your happiness off to some vague destination of completeness in the future. You can be happy right now just knowing that you have made some progress. Think to yourself, *little by little, I'm generating momentum. I'm making progress.* More so than robotic task-completion, what life is really about is having fun and enjoying each day as it comes.

Stop Over-Delegating

Many of the time management books out there will emphasize the importance of delegating. And to a large extent, I don't disagree with that because there is undoubtedly enormous power and value in delegating tasks to other people. With that said, however, in today's society the scale is tipped too much towards delegation and too far away from taking action.

Have you ever come across someone who I like to call a *whiteboard hero?* These are the kinds of people who love to talk about projects, delegating tasks left and right, spending hours drawing diagrams and figures on the whiteboard, but they never actually get anything done. If all someone is going to do is write on the whiteboard, they are wasting people's time. Don't misunderstand: there is value in meetings, taking notes, and discussing tasks. In fact, there is value in using a whiteboard when someone is effectively facilitating a meeting or learning session. I'm just saying – not in a derogatory way, but in a simple statement of fact and truth – there are people out there who would prefer to endlessly write on a whiteboard than to ever take action. If you're the CEO of your company, then yes, you've 100% earned the privilege to facilitate and delegate. But 99% of us aren't CEOs and 99% of us should have at least some stake in helping do the work that completes a project.

When faced with a task, ask yourself: is this something you are better off doing yourself? Would you save yourself time by not delegating it and instead just zeroing in and knocking it off? Is it one of your strengths that you are uniquely qualified to focus on and achieve? If not, then, by all means, delegate the task if that's an option, but take time to consider the possibility that it's something you're better off completing yourself.

Favor Simplicity

I was recently chatting on Skype with my friend Rick Woods, The Functional Organizer. He is a professional organizer as well as a professional speaker, author, and consultant. Here are Rick's insights as he talks about the power of simplicity:

> Create a master to-do list to write down all of your goals, tasks, projects, and aspirations. Then create a short daily to-do list pulled from the master to-do list. Keep it simple and have the short daily to-do list have just a couple of things on it. If you get two important things done every day, that's ten important things done a week, which equates to somewhere around 500 important things done in a year – accounting for vacations and holidays. When it comes to meetings, I've found that big meetings are bad and small meetings are good. And when you have small meetings, keep them short.

Rick speaks on time management, and his insights are brilliant. Here are some other extremely powerful tips from Rick:

- If you have a bad start to your day, it doesn't mean you can't have a great ending to your day.

- Get conscious about who you are spending your time with and make it a point to surround yourself with the right people (a big part of reaching your Mountaintop is to get around the right people, as John told us earlier in the chapter; you could be doing everything right, but if you are around the wrong people they will bring you down).

- Work on always getting just a little bit better. Try new things and see if you can make small improvements each day. The tendency is to want to change everything at once, but that's overwhelming. It's those small, daily, and consistent changes that lead to real, lasting shifts in your life. Yes, there are times when you need to make massive leaps forward, but consistency and daily action is key.

- Build momentum by checking things off of your to-do list. Rather than feeling bad about not getting everything done, feel good about getting those one or two things done that really matter.

- Check your email in 3-hour increments. Rather than mindlessly checking it all day every day, try reducing your email time to a three times per day, and then from there down to once per day.

Chatting with Rick on Skype several times over a period of a year, I was amazed by his superb knowledge. See what I mean about getting around the right people? Whenever I was done talking to Rick, I always felt better than I had previously, with more motivation and focus toward getting what matters most complete. He is a top-notch time manager, and he is so centered, peaceful, and calm.

"Don't rush through tasks, as you might miss some things," Rick said. "Enjoy each activity and make it an end unto itself. This will also allow you to develop the skill of concentration, which is learnable.

"The key is to get your content flowing and to get into the flow state of mind," Rick stated. "Don't wait until the time feels just right. Instead, start today and watch as kernels of insight come out of what you are doing. The beauty of momentum is that even if you're busy, you'll find the time to get things done. You'll still squeeze it into those 15-minute segments. Also, don't look at the time. Clock-watching will take your focus off of what you're doing. The best days and jobs are the ones where you are not looking at the time at all because you are letting time naturally pass while you do your thing.

"If possible, take social media notifications off of your phone. It's perfectly alright to check social media, as many of us do, but don't do it all day. Check it consciously at certain time periods each day and stay in control of your social media habits.

"Lastly, be loose with your goals," Rick said. "If you 100% know what you want, by all means, go after it with full speed. But also, don't tie yourself to a goal if it's not what you really want to do."

This was incredibly liberating to hear because I realized that yes, many of my goals are 100% set in stone, but many of my goals are evolving. For example, I'm a big traveler and even though not all people in the world see the relevance of travel to what I do as a speaker, it's a big part of me and not something I'm going to give up doing just because someone doesn't see the point of it. To me, travel is life! The perspective, the friendship, the eye-opening experiences from my world travels are all priceless, and I will continue to travel until the day I die.

To tie this back to the last chapter, helping people (especially high school and college students) get through challenging times is still my number one focus. With that said, speaking requires frequent travel; I also often use weekends to jet off to a new city or location. I love using my free time to travel. When you have multiple goals and passions, there are win-win solutions.

A lot of people like to turn life into black and white, but that's not the way it works. Who says I can't travel *and* be a speaker? In fact, many speakers do just that! I know many people who also have an innate love for travel. Don't let other people place limits on you. As Randy Gage says, "don't ever let someone else's limiting beliefs become yours." Create your own reality and seek win-win solutions to your biggest challenges. While it's not my main focus, I do guest blogging for 1000traveltips.com, and I speak at travel conferences, sharing my budget travel expertise with the world. I recently spoke at the Travel Adventure Show in Philadelphia and it was a wonderful experience. I met a lot of new people and I did it on a weekend so it didn't take away from my main focus. There's nothing wrong with this because it doesn't detract from other areas of my business. The truth is, these side endeavors add great enrichment and pleasure to my life.

Rick's insights are powerful, and he's a master of his craft. I don't know about you, but I'm going to follow his advice! I can't emphasize enough that reaching your Mountaintop is reaching YOUR version of success and doing what you want to do, regardless of what others think, say, or do. As Joel Osteen, a speaker, bestselling author, and inspirational preacher says, "others have every right to share with you their opinion – and you have every right not to listen to that opinion."

I am drilling this point home with you because when you put this book down and go back to living your life, the world will once again inundate you with all sorts of "should's" and "have to's". You definitely don't want to cancel all of your commitments suddenly, but over time you can take back control of your life. Remember what Jenny Drescher taught us? Get rid of the "should's" and start focusing on what you want to do.

Live your own life and stop letting others dictate to you what you should and shouldn't do.

These are amazing insights from Rick, aren't they? Notice Rick's tips have a common theme: simplicity. Create space in your life. Get rid of the clutter. Donate books you've read and don't need anymore. Say no to activities and obligations that don't serve your greater purpose. The extra space you create in your life by being true to yourself will allow you to make a magnificent impact on the world.

Do What Matters

My 53-year-old aunt was in the hospital undergoing life-threatening surgery (sadly, she's passed away now – I was very close with her) and my mom had to take care of my cousin, my aunt's son. I was asked, last-minute, to spend time with my little brother who is a freshman in high school because my dad went to the hospital to be with my aunt, his sister. My little brother is a smart kid and would have been fine on his own, but my parents wanted me to drive down from my apartment to be with him because it was an extremely difficult time for our family and they didn't want my little brother to be left alone.

For that afternoon and evening, I had a number of important things planned. I was looking forward to attending a networking event that some key players in my industry were attending. In addition, I had several overdue errands to run and an important upcoming speech to prepare for. I had even just blocked out some time to work on writing my next book. Listen, I know no one ever wants bad news, and I don't want to sound distracted because I'm a friendly and understanding person, but this was a particularly difficult night to have this come up.

Thankfully, I had my values and priorities in order, and I knew that my little brother came first. So I drove down from my apartment to Newtown, Connecticut, picked him up, and spontaneously took him to a New York Rangers hockey game at Madison Square Garden. While taking the metro-north train down into the city from Connecticut, I realized something important:

It's essential to have your values and priorities in place because time management is more than getting everything done as quickly as possible – what it's really about is doing what matters.

It ended up being a great night, and I'm absolutely 100% sure my late aunt would have been proud of us for having fun, enjoying the moment, and taking our minds off of the stress (something she always taught us to do). I know she's smiling from somewhere as I write this.

Reward Yourself

I'm a bit tired. But more than feeling tired, I'm also feeling burned out. Writing this chapter was the last thing I felt like doing. But you know what? I wrote it anyway. I realized that I didn't want to put this off any longer. I also understood that, as my friend Chip Janiszewski, of

Happiness and Success GPS, said to me over breakfast one morning, "the present moment is all you ever really have." In a very realistic and practical way, the present moment is all that exists in life. Chip is a smart and successful speaker and trainer. What he says makes sense.

"*Sameville*, as I like to call it," Chip said, "is where most people live. It's choosing to let other opinions and society influence you. My number one focus when coaching, communicating, and working with others is a message of awareness. You can choose to be happy, to grab a positive mindset, and do whatever you want with your life."

What Chip is saying here is that if an external focus dictates your life, you'll never find the time to work on your purpose effectively. Look at the big picture view of your life and remember that properly managing your time is really managing your life, priorities, and true goals. This includes being your own best friend and knowing when to take a break or vacation.

Train yourself to be disciplined – it's a learnable skill. When you are disciplined and do what you told yourself you would do, reward yourself. Whether that reward is watching a movie or TV show, eating a delicious meal, grabbing ice cream, laying down on the couch, or even traveling somewhere new, you will feel great about yourself on the way to your destination.

When in doubt, listen to San Francisco 49ers wide receiver legend Jerry Rice's words of wisdom. I shared this quote in the second chapter, and it's so powerful I'll share it again: "Today I will do what others won't, so tomorrow I can accomplish what others can't." This does NOT mean to do everything suddenly and burn yourself out. What it means is to establish a consistent, daily schedule and routine to make periodic, incremental progress, so that tomorrow, next week, next month, and next year you can do things that you can only dream about today.

Embrace Your Challenges

Revolutionizing your life through the power of time management is not about running away from your problems; it's about facing them directly. Let's hear more from Chip, an incredibly inspiring man.

"I know we all have different relationships going on," Chip said, "and we all deal with peer pressure as far as ways we are expected to spend our time. But we need to knock ourselves out of *Sameville* as fast as possible because it's not sane to live below our potential, endlessly trying to please others. When I'm presenting, I'll often show a STOP sign to help people awaken to themselves. Then I'll go into the foundational positive mindset."

This could be a whole book unto itself, but for the sake of simplicity, I'll boil Chip's foundational tactics into four steps for you. I want to make sure you can begin applying this in your life immediately:

1. Look forward to life each day. Wake up in gratitude and thank your lucky stars for being alive.

2. Make sure there is a purpose and a *why* behind every thought, word, and action. Make a list of all the reasons why you want to achieve something.

3. Create a strategic plan, an outline of where you're going, and the steps you need to implement to make it happen.

4. Take massive, focused, determined, and consistent action. Remember, everyone in the world has

dreams, but the exceptional and above-average person puts those dreams into action.

As you climb your Mountaintop, it's incredibly easy to forget any one, or a combination, of these four points. When we get lost in the minutiae, it's easy to be frazzled and not remind ourselves what we're grateful for. When our determination and persistence is running thin, our *why* will carry us through the bumps in the road.

When we've lost sight of the forest and are lost in the trees, our strategic plan will lead us back to the next rung of the ladder. And when we know a lot of success tactics but aren't applying anything, massive action will push us forward.

"That's incredibly helpful," I said to Chip. "And I'm sure many would agree. The challenge is finding money. Many people don't have a lot of money and after going through setbacks myself, I know what it's like to be counting pennies," I said. "I agree with what you are saying here; it's great. One of the main messages of this book is that money is only one small metric of success, so you hit the nail on the head here. And managing your time requires far more discipline than it does money. At the same time, money is a big obstacle for many in getting started."

"If money is your goal, then you'll never be happy," Chip said. "In the process I teach, which involves establishing a positive foundational mindset, and creating a purpose, along with writing down reasons why you do what you do, you literally don't need any money to get started. I'm all for the grind, the hard work, the struggle, the counting pennies. I'm just saying that when you implement this process, it will allow you to stop settling for far less than what you truly deserve."

I nodded, soaking in his thoughts. When you implement Chip's process, that's when your time management will improve because you'll have your eye on your goals instead of your eye on the distractions.

"It's a great point, Jeff," Chip continued. "I run a group meeting myself, and I help others get through all sorts of challenges. I get it, I really do. I've had all sorts of struggles and setbacks in my life. The key is to focus on the good, not the bad, because what you focus on expands. Sounds incredibly simple, but there are countless negative people who are obsessed with the bad and won't focus on the good. That's why my purpose in life is to help people wake up each day happy, fulfilled, and ready to give their gifts and talents in service to others."

"I love it," I said. "If you are focused on the bad and filled with negativity, then even the best time management strategies won't work. That's why you must get your mind right first."

"Exactly. Keep your focus off of the negativity and the people who want to pull you down," Chip said. "Looping back to the *Sameville* thing, since it's so important to be aware of, the way I live my purpose is by reminding people over and over again that they have *the power of choice*. Everything you do is based on your mindset. The tendency for people is to want to jump straight to doing. But if they haven't first made a plan and gotten their mindset in order, the right action won't be taking place."

Time management is all about making sure that you've leaned your ladder against the right wall. This book is about both going after your own version of success and taking practical action; something Chip embodies to a tee.

What Can You Do Right Now?

Entrepreneur and life coach Michelle Demers has some great additional insight for us. Once you have your ladder leaned up against the right wall, you must refuse to stand still. As Will Rogers said, "Even if you're on the right track, you'll get run over if you just sit there." Michelle explained to me that having goals, visions, and plans is great; it's an excellent starting point. At the same time, it's also essential to focus on what you can do *this day, right now*, as you make your climb.

Someone she knew hiked the Appalachian Trail. He had the vision, the plan, the map, and the stages. But most importantly, every day when he woke up the only thing he told himself he had to do was go the next ten miles that day. He broke his huge goal into tiny behaviors and habits. On a daily basis, this man was looking at the next leg of his journey. He didn't overwhelm himself with the whole project and instead focused on what he could do right now: one mile, one step at a time.

The point Michelle makes through this powerful analogy is that you can only do one segment, one thing at a time. As Eckhart Tolle says, "the only thing ever real about your journey is the step you are taking at this moment."

"If you are thinking about the whole *shebang* in a day," Michelle said, "and you get some blisters, and it's rainy, and it sucks while having a bad day, you may think, *OK, I'm not doing this for the next 200 days*."

Here's what Michelle is excited to tell you as you take life one day at a time: **if you break down those larger**

activities into the tiniest, minute-by-minute, action steps, then even the biggest monster is capable of being conquered.

There is wisdom in coming into the present moment and taking one small, purposeful step forward. The step you take in this present moment is all you need to focus on. Like Michael Benner taught us, keep your focus off of the past and future as much as you can. Embrace the moment, enjoy the process, and reward yourself along the way.

What's Your One Thing?

Remember Geeta Nadkarni from Chapter 2, the Mountaintop Mindset? I met her when she was speaking at the 2015 National Speakers Association conference. She has some powerful thoughts on managing your time that act as the perfect summary of some of the best points in this chapter:

> When managing your time, ask: what are the most essential pieces to the puzzle of what you're trying to accomplish? Instead of having thirty things on my list, I'll have ONE thing on my list. It's not easy to do, but when you apply this, you'll be able to get the vital few one or two tasks done each day. When I take on too much, I become overwhelmed, and my decision-making becomes poorer, so how you manage your time affects every aspect of your life.

Geeta went on to tell me that she hired someone who is more structure-oriented than she is (Geeta is creative-oriented). Geeta will do the brainstorming and then have her partner give her ONE task to do; she's then not allowed to touch anything until she gets that one thing done.

"Then I feel good," Geeta said, "and can reward myself along the way. The truth is there's often only ONE thing you need to do when the tendency is to think everything is important."

Geeta is a huge success and, like John Lee Dumas and Rick Woods, her insights make sense. She just described a powerful tactic: collaborate with people who have strengths in your areas of weakness. Focus on your strengths. Develop areas you are not strong in. And get help from people who know more than you do about a certain skill or topic.

Back Yourself Into a Corner

If you are still finding a hard time getting started or effectively managing your time with all that you have to do, try doing what prosperity expert and successful author Randy Gage suggests: back yourself into a corner.

"When I know I have to get a big project done, but I'm putting it off, I'll back myself into a corner by not only setting up a deadline but getting other people to rely and count on that deadline," Randy said. "When I know that other people are counting on me, even when I don't want or feel like working on it, I'll kick into gear and get the project done."

You don't want to overpromise anything to anyone, so find the balance that works for you and apply this strategy when appropriate. With that said, this can be incredibly effective when used appropriately. If you are still finding yourself stuck, back yourself into a corner and force yourself to make progress on the task at hand.

It's an Ongoing Process

The improvement of your time management is an ongoing process and will improve as you grow as a leader. Some days will be wonderful, and you will feel like you're in the flow. Other days, your energy levels will dip, and you will struggle to focus and get things done. The important thing is not to get caught up on any particular good or bad day, but to simply keep marching forward and making progress.

There are entire books devoted to time management because it's an important subject. I knew this topic was crucial to share with you because it will enable you to navigate the hectic demands and stressors of life better while you overcome obstacles and revolutionize your life. I've been studying time management for years and have done several seminars on it – what I did here is consolidate the best and most powerful aspects of time management into one chapter by featuring some of the world's top experts on the subject.

Don't try to change everything at once. Take one tip from this chapter and begin today.

Questions for Reflection

1. What are some bottlenecks in your schedule and time? How can you reduce these obstacles?

2. What are some activities or commitments you have a false sense of obligation toward? If they aren't the best use of your time, how can you respectfully transition out of these commitments?

3. What one project or task would, upon completion, fill you with the greatest sense of meaning, purpose, and power?

Chapter 8: The Soft Skills are the Hard Skills

"At the end of the day, remember that pain is healthy. Pain is a good thing. Pain reminds us of where we don't want to go again. Pain shakes us awake."
— Brian Olds

I spoke with Brian Olds, social entrepreneur, master networker, professional speaker, and radio show host on a bitter cold, mid-February, Sunday afternoon in Baltimore, Maryland, at a diner off of Eastern Avenue on the outskirts of the city. I originally met him through Toastmasters while I was living in Baltimore and he's turned into a lifelong friend. I traveled to Baltimore to meet in person with him, and it was well worth the four-and-a-half- to five-hour drive, because I absolutely love meeting face-to-face with others – especially with my good friend Brian. I teach others the importance of meeting with people face-to-face, and I can genuinely say I live my message.

"I'm doing a purge right now in my life," Brian said as he sat and we started talking. "Simplifying, reducing, and focusing in on my most important goals. So this conversation comes at the perfect time."

Brian is an entrepreneur, having created the organization called SKILLS, which stands for Sharing Knowledge and Information for Lifelong Success. He hosts a radio show, does events/seminars, actively speaks in the community, and *passionately* enjoys sharing practical knowledge, insight, and advice with the world. He also frequently connects business professionals with one another, taking the focus off of himself by helping others further their career. My friends, please know this man does it all, and he's in his early thirties.

What I love so much about Brian is that he's one of the most humble and sincere guys you will ever meet. He does so much for others but never takes the credit. For example, I was getting an enormous amount of rejections when I was looking for a publisher for my first book. I finally found a publisher because of a connection I made at one of Brian's SKILLS events. The woman I met connected me with a publisher she knew. I hit it off with the publishing company, and the rest is history.

I thanked Brian profusely for being such a big motivator and inspiration in my life.

"I just acted as a conduit," Brian said. "You're the one who saw the opportunity and ran with it. It's all you."

The truth is, Brian has helped many people succeed in life. He's a true social entrepreneur because he cares about the well-being of others from the bottom of his heart.

Brian's core belief, and a big reason why he is so successful, is that when one person succeeds, everyone succeeds.

"A rising tide lifts all the boats in the harbor," Brian added.

Only one word I have to say to that: WOW. You don't have to think in terms of constant competition. You can think in terms of mutually beneficial solutions like Brian does.

SKILLS

"Tell me more about SKILLS," I said. "You've done so much with this organization."

"Initially I got a bunch of people together for a fundraiser for Morgan State University Toastmasters and more people showed up than I ever would have imagined," Brian said. "I didn't end up using SKILLS as a fundraising organization, but given the level of interest I was able to create in a relatively short period of time, I thought *wow, this could be something.*

"This happened in 2010. I knew I wanted to create something that would fill the gap in knowledge and skills that I perceived there to be for newer and younger professionals. In other words, folks who are graduating who have book knowledge like math, science, accounting, and other forms of general and important knowledge, but who don't know the soft skills like how to effectively build relationships. These are the skills needed to be successful in life, and they were sort of glazed over in school. The purpose of SKILLS is to fill that gap," Brian shared.

"That's excellent and is really the perfect reason to create the organization," I said. "This is amazing because it ties perfectly into the message I'm looking to get across with this book. It's about learning the right skills to reach your Mountaintop, your version of success. These are skills no one ever shared with me in school, so I wholeheartedly agree they are often glazed over or not covered at all. So would you say soft skills like communication are *more* important than hard skills like book knowledge?"

"That's a great question," Brian said. "Without a doubt, book knowledge is an essential foundation that is needed to do well in certain professions. **But the soft stuff is really the hard stuff, so I hesitate to call them 'soft skills.'** For example, people with strong technical talent who have awesome engineering knowledge are off to a great start, but in order to advance and do well in their career, they're going to need more than that.

"Regardless of what industry you are in, the soft stuff is the hard stuff. Being able to negotiate, size up other individuals, lead, communicate, stay productive, and properly manage time. Those skills help you to be a better you and make those around you better. Those are the skills that matter," Brian explained.

"I agree," I said. "I'm all for hard skills, and when I was in college and graduate school you'd see no one hitting the books harder than me, but there's a whole other set of skills that often means the difference between success and failure."

"Yes, well said," Brian replied. "The minimum to get you in the door are the programming skills, the SEO, the marketing – whatever skills are specific to each person's desired industry and career choice. However, to really make an impact, you have to be able to influence and persuade other people."

Are you as excited as I am to hear more from Brian? This guy is the real deal.

Enjoy Your Life While Achieving Your Goals

"A lot of people get stressed out in the process of achieving their goals and making a transition into doing what they want," I said. "It's also tough to make that daily climb, with so many distractions. Is there any way around that?" I asked.

"Your goals should be aligned with those activities that you're doing every day that bring you some level of fulfillment and enjoyment," Brian said. "Your goal shouldn't be some far off thing that happens at some predetermined time in the future. When your head hits the pillow, you need to think, *wow, I did one thing today, and that one thing moved me towards my goal*.

"The concept of enjoyment," Brian continued, "should be examined a little closer. People feel most fulfilled when they accomplish something. Yes, vacation is good for relaxing. But you get that natural shot of norepinephrine when you get that feeling of achievement. The point is, fulfillment and happiness come from feeling valued, to seeing your dream come to life a little bit at a time.

"You should feel valued," Brian continued. "If NOT, look at the dashboard of your life just like you look at the dashboard of a car. The dashboard provides indicators that something is wrong. If the check engine light comes on, but you don't know what exactly it may be – for example, you are not fulfilled – then go under the hood and check it out. That could include reflection, meditation, introspection, dialogue with close family members/friends, and things of that sort. When you ignore the check engine light for too long, you break down on the side of the road. For some people, this could be 20 years after the initial check engine light came on and they wonder what the heck happened, but the truth is they never checked under the hood."

"That's incredibly powerful stuff, Brian," I said. "I'm so excited to share this."

"Remember that pain can be a good thing, too," Brian said. "Because it shakes us awake and reminds us where not to go. We want to enjoy life while achieving our goals, but we also want to remember that pain has a purpose and can be beneficial in its own way. That's why we must face our challenges directly."

Multi-tasking is a Myth

"I've interviewed some experts on time management," I said, "and I can't help but ask you while I have you here, as you are an expert as well – what are the best ways to manage your time, especially when managing challenges and constraints?"

"For me," Brian articulated, "time management is all about avoiding redundancy whenever possible. At the micro level, avoiding redundancy is having the appropriate systems in place to capture, share, and retrieve information as quickly as possible. Do the things today that will save you time tomorrow.

"Evernote is perfect because it syncs everything for you. One key that helps me a lot is to process most things right then and there. Most people put things into the 'will do' pile and then never get to it. But if you focus on one thing at a time, you can plow through lots of work. Tim Ferriss calls it single-handling. Just touch things once if possible, and then be done with it.

"We have such an absurd amount of things going on at once," Brian added, "that it can be hard to know what to take action on when making the climb. Text messages, meetings, bumping into people we know, action items from meetings, emails, phone calls: some of these inputs are immediately actionable, and some of these inputs are questions that need to be asked or decisions that need to be made. For some inputs, you may have no idea what to do, and for other inputs, you may have projects in motion with multiple steps behind them.

"Here's the key to remember," Brian added. "Multi-tasking is a myth. The brain can only focus on one thing at a time. There's a cognitive penalty for switching from one thing to another (even if only for a few seconds). We all have about 21 projects going on, give or take. You have to think about archiving certain projects and then giving your full attention and focus to your most desired goal. After a couple months of work, it is easy to forget about these other side projects. But if you are organized and on top of your folders/documents you can retrieve what you need in the future. Get all of your ideas down so you can clear your mind. Only then will you be able to give your full energy and attention to that one thing that could change your life."

Brian's insights serve to give you that added reminder and push to stay *really* focused.

Parting Words of Wisdom

"The soft stuff is the hard stuff," Brian reiterated. "We need more people who aren't afraid to be themselves. It's important they TRULY be themselves, giving themselves the permission to tap into the thing that got them excited when they were five years old. I say this because I am allowing myself to be vulnerable here. I grew up watching cartoons like Gargoyles, excited about science, technology, engineering, and space shuttle launches.

"I don't think my calling is to be an engineer, but I know I need to be tapped into that area at some level," Brian communicated. "If I didn't end up getting a scholarship to go to college, I would have gone into the Air Force. **It doesn't matter what you do professionally, that bliss inside you is always there. You won't be truly happy, fulfilled, and enjoying the journey until you have embraced that and given yourself permission to be the person you're meant to be.**

"As a corollary to that, I've noticed that a lot of books say, *hey, you need to make this massive change*, but I don't think that's the case. In a lot of cases, there is an opportunity to tap into your authentic self within what you are already doing. You don't have to quit your job; you don't even have to start a business. If it leads to these things, then that's great. But the truth is that the world needs people to be their authentic self.

"It doesn't matter if you are a receptionist, a janitor, a waiter, or any other kind of profession – when you give yourself permission to be your authentic self, the outcome is not replicable anywhere on the entire planet," Brian continued. "For example, I recently witnessed a woman cutting meat at Shoppers ask the person in front of me in line why she ordered what she ordered.

"After receiving an answer the woman cutting the meat went on to say, 'You know, we have this other type of ham with less sodium that will perfectly meet your needs.' I stood there thinking, *wow, I've never seen anyone get consultative advice about lunch meat.* That person wasn't just doing a job; they were bringing their full selves into what they do. When you are authentically you, then the promotion, marketing, and growth – all those things we want – naturally occur.

"When your head hits the pillow, you want to think, *ok, this was a great day, and I can't wait for tomorrow.* The days when I think, *wow, what a great day*, were the days when I had a meeting the morning after not wanting to get out of bed. I was stretched out of my comfort zone and allowed myself to operate on the fringe of fear long enough to do what was required on that day," Brian said.

"From the outside looking in," Brian further explained, "someone could be like, *oh, that's not that scary*. But when you are in the middle of it all, it's a lot. And it's scary. You know you are heading in the right direction when you are a slightly better version of yourself than when you took your head off the pillow that morning. And this only happens when we have genuine opportunities for growth.

"If something is not working, re-examine it. Continue to reflect. Take time out to give yourself a breather so that you can unwind, enjoy life, and process everything," Brian said.

Simply invaluable and incredibly helpful words from Brian. They will help us as we continue to move forward and reach our Mountaintop.

Questions for Reflection

1. What "soft" skill is your weak point? What organization can you join to improve your communication and leadership skills? Toastmasters? Kiwanis? Lions? Rotary?

2. What indicator is on in the dashboard of your life right now? What area of your life needs to be more closely examined?

3. What activity caused you joy and bliss as a child? How can you reconnect with this childlike sense of wonder, imagination, purpose, hope, and possibility?

Chapter 9: Make an Impact by Being of Service to Others

"The best way to find yourself
is to lose yourself in the service of others."
– Mahatma Gandhi

Let's now get into ways you can really make a long-lasting impact, leave your mark, and reach your Mountaintop. While you are thinking about where you want to be three to five years from now and beyond, you also need to be fully in the present moment and embracing the resources you have available NOW.

While there are certainly going to be ups and downs along the way, progress and setbacks, you can learn to funnel unwanted situations into something bigger and better. I use the dysfunction I experienced in the past as a way to help high school and college students around the world. What difficult circumstance have you been through that you can use for added motivation to reach your Mountaintop?

Remember, one of the goals of this book is, in some way, to flip on its head what you've heard about success in the past. **Reaching your Mountaintop is not about trying to impress and please others. It's not about worrying what others think. It's not about fitting into society's standards. It's about being your quintessential, authentic self in each and every moment by seeking to serve and help others.**

You win by making other people feel good about themselves. You get back at your critics not by engaging them and lowering yourself to their level, but by being kind to them. You win by living such a happy, successful, and

177

service-filled life that your critics are left stunned and speechless. Become so focused on serving others and doing good that you don't have time for negativity.

Of course, this is ultimately not about winning or losing, or "getting back" at anyone. But when you go for the gold and reach your Mountaintop, there will be some good people and some bad people around you. Some may even be liars and betrayers. Some may not be directly mean to your face, but they may not have your best interests at heart. It's important to watch out for people like this.

Throughout this book, we've discussed some important and powerful tips to achieve what you want. The catch-22 is that when you are reaching your fullest potential and at your best, you are most often *serving others*. This is not just a figure of speech nor is it something to which we are paying lip service. It means genuinely helping others and keeping the focus on what you can do for them.

One of the key aspects of success is not to be so concerned about what others think, good or bad. Don't get attached to other people's opinions. The successful and inspiring man we are about to hear from, John Powers, told me once, "You don't have to care what other people think." He is the perfect example of serving others. He's so busy helping those in need that he doesn't even have time to worry about what other people think of him. Ironically, people respect and love him for that.

There's power in serving others. The greatest achievement of all is when you are focused on providing value to others.

I thought I had a lot going on until I met John. I've had a tendency sometimes to bite off more than I can chew. And I've always had an absurdly involved schedule. But then I met John, my former manager at Acara Partners and good friend – a true champion, man of integrity and character, and role model for us all. He's one of the most involved people I've ever met, and he truly put things into perspective for me!

A Powerful and Meaningful Service Project: Quality Over Quantity

In addition to being a director of communications at Acara, John is a college professor at Quinnipiac who is actively pursuing his Ph.D. He is a leader of a semiannual service endeavor which we'll hear about in a moment. He travels often and has a wonderful family with whom he spends a lot of time. This man does it all.

Johns leads an important service project to help people who are less fortunate – people with little to no money, food, and/or shelter. He travels down to the Dominican Republic twice a year with a large group of awesome people that include students, volunteers, people from his church, and people from other areas of his life as well. (For example, I went on the service trip in June of 2015, and I knew John through where we used to work together. I had a blast and made some good friends and contacts through the experience while helping others.)

I found it fascinating and incredible how John turned a simple thought of helping others into well over two decades of service to people in the Dominican Republic, with now hundreds of people involved, so I asked him more about how it all got started.

"It all started when I was 23 years old and recently married," John said. "My wife and I posed a simple yet powerful question to one another: *What can we do to help others, other than sending money?*"

There's absolutely nothing wrong with sending money to charitable organizations, but they wanted to do something more personal and make a truly meaningful impact. Keeping their eyes and ears open for a chance to do this, they heard of an opportunity from people at their church to travel south to the Dominican Republic. It was serendipitous in the sense that it started as nothing more than an idea and conversation, but John and his wife were serious about taking action to help those in need.

In February of 1990, they went on their first trip to the Dominican Republic. They went there for a week and saw the vast need. They witnessed firsthand the poverty and suffering many of the Dominicans had to go through on a daily basis, and it broke their hearts.

When John and his wife returned home from their first trip, they made an important decision. They could have gone to places like Haiti and Nicaragua, but they decided to commit to this one project in the Dominican Republic. Remember what we talked about as far as focusing in on your one thing?

"Let's make a BIG difference with this one project," John said. "And then we can expand from there."

Let's now fast forward twenty-six years later, to the year 2016. John now goes every year, multiple times a year, and has been to the Dominican Republic over fifty times. He chose to go back to the same place every year because having an impact means building relationships; it also means seeing what you have worked on over the years and observing the progress.

When I was in the Dominican Republic in June of 2015, I saw that they had built *entire buildings.* Do you know how much that helps people? An incredible amount! And this is only one small example of the huge impact John and his team have made in this community. When I was down there, I helped build a home for a family that was homeless. I couldn't have been happier to do it.

If John and his wife went to the Dominican Republic once and left, they would've not made as meaningful and deep of an impact as they could have. True service and reaching your Mountaintop is about quality and depth, not about getting something done just for the sake of completion. Know that if you go somewhere once and never again, it's still wonderful that you made a difference. However, the over-arching point here is how John, his wife, and their team have made a **sustained and long-lasting commitment to what they are doing to help others.**

For example, starting in 1990, John and his team helped build a hospital from scratch, and it's now a fully operational facility. Can you imagine living somewhere with no doctors or hospitals? John identified a problem and then filled the need with a solution. When John returns to the Dominican twice each year, he marvels at how far the area has come over the last twenty-five years while he continues to do more work. The one village (Batey 50, in La Romana) is now a model for other villages. This same mindset applies to doing all types of service projects.

"Get specific in where you are helping people and get to know others," John said. "The beauty of going with a group is that you get to choose where you focus your efforts. You can find your niche and put all of your energy into helping a specific group of people or assisting with a certain project or initiative."

In Batey 50, there are schools, houses, water filters, medical clinics, and all kinds of buildings and projects with which one may assist. There are now more than 2,000 Americans who go to the Dominican every year. Isn't it amazing how something so big has come from something so small? That's the power in reaching your Mountaintop – both serving others and enlisting others in your project by getting them involved. That's leadership. That's impact. That's legacy.

Different Ways to Make a Difference

Further discussing his Dominican service experience, John told me how other people in the Batey 50 village come and help the Americans. These extremely poor and poverty-stricken Dominicans have nothing material to give, but they come over and show their support by giving their time. This led John to share an important realization with us:

If you can't give money, you can always give time.

"Sometimes just showing up and showing you care by truly listening to people...that's huge," John said. "People are always so concerned about the money. And yes, money is important, but the core of service is the human connection. Go volunteer at a soup kitchen, help serve the meal, and actually talk to the people you are serving. Sometimes talking to people is just as powerful as giving them money, if not more so, because they need to know somebody cares.

"Many Dominicans have no civilization, no communication, no means of really anything, and then here comes a bus full of Americans," John emphasized.

"When they see us showing up they go crazy, in a good way, because it gives them hope. They will talk about us to others. They will go home and tell family, friends, and classmates about the initiatives going on in Batey 50. Other people will then get involved as awareness spreads."

John is a realistic, intelligent, thoughtful man and he knows that everyone won't be able to do service projects in other countries. But you can still make an impact at home.

"The thing to remember," John said, "is that the same hopelessness we see in the Dominican Republic exists in our very own towns and cities. Some people feel forgotten," John continued. "These are people who made mistakes, but they're human just like us. All you need to do is show that you care."

Caring about others is crucial here. The challenges and setbacks I had in high school would have been a lot easier if I had felt like someone at my high school actually cared about what I was going through. When you listen to others and encourage them in any setting, you are serving others. What I experienced in my younger years is something I can now laugh about, but the point is that caring about an individual not only makes a difference but can literally save their life.

John has a great head on his shoulders, to say the least. Sadly, so few people on this planet care about genuinely helping others that when you show you care, you stand out. The heart and soul of service is showing others that you care. When you do this, you make them feel like a million bucks, and you pull them out of despair. Imagine how good it would feel to help people each and every day by giving them hope. This is one of the keys to making it to your Mountaintop.

If you are occupied with a hectic and demanding schedule, start small. Smile at someone. Lend a listening ear. Silently send someone a blessing. You don't have to be recognized by others for your efforts. It's about putting your inner life before your outer life. Inner power is much stronger than outer recognition.

Reaching your Mountaintop is the exception, not the rule, but if we get this content in enough hands, it doesn't have to be that way anymore.

Community and Perspective

Remember that huge hospital I mentioned John and his team created? He didn't just create a useful building, though that was monumental unto itself – he also played a role in establishing a powerful and interactive community. People who run the hospital and church in Batey 50 (the village they've chosen to help) are absolutely insistent that each Dominican works and helps out. No one gets a free pass.

There's no welfare in a place like this, so everyone comes and helps. They must rely on one another. If there is a school being built for their kids, then you can bet your bottom dollar that the families are helping push the wheelbarrow. There is no tolerance for laziness, swindling, and greed. They do sympathize with people (there are always exceptions to the rule, like people who have disabilities), but there is absolutely zero tolerance for people trying to take advantage of the system.

With that said, this system works. It creates an atmosphere of total expectations and each person knows without the least shred of doubt they must contribute value to both the specific project and the community overall.

Every family must get involved and be a part of the process. They are grateful for the help they receive from John's group and shower them with gratitude and appreciation.

"Seeing all of this," I said, "what's your perspective on life?"

"People just don't realize what these people in this part of the Dominican are going through," John said. "It's easy to come back to the United States and forget all about their hardship. One week you are saving someone's life and the next week you are mad because Netflix isn't loading. We joke about first world problems, but there are people with no healthcare and no job opportunities in places like the Dominican Republic. These are hardworking, family-oriented, and really good people who just haven't been given a fair shake at life."

The most tragic part of all is that many of these people are trapped in their situation.

"These people can't move and are trapped," John said. "They have families, they have no money, and they have nowhere else to go. They have one skill and that's to cut sugarcane with a machete. That's why it's absolutely crucial that we give people opportunities to live, work, and provide for their families."

And that's why John does what he does. As a man with an enormous amount of perspective, he can help thousands of people through his service projects. It's very hard to imagine what some of these Dominicans have to go through on a daily basis, but John and his team are there to help as much as they possibly can.

Remember what we discussed way back at the beginning of the book? When facing your own challenges and situations in life, John suggests you ask:

Is this really a problem?

Look at your current situation from the eyes of what some of the most unfortunate people on this planet are going through. Please know that this is by no means whatsoever putting down your problem or disregarding it – you definitely need to honor what's wrong, deal with it, and fix the situation (don't let other people marginalize what you're going through as you solve your challenges). It's just a way of applying a situational mindset that allows you to handle the ups and downs of life better without losing your cool or going into the dumps.

I say this with a smile now, knowing all is well, and I apply John's lessons in my life every day. But a decade ago when I experienced the worst moment of my life after getting cut from my baseball team – what you read in the first chapter – I didn't know any of these strategies or insights. As small as that was in the grand scheme of things, and as much as I can laugh about it now, baseball was my *life,* and as a college recruit athlete, it was a devastating blow to unexpectedly not make the team. That's why I'm so passionate about getting this material into the hands of as many people as possible. I now know strong relationships and perspective can turn a nightmare situation into a positive learning experience. Had I been friends with John when I was seventeen, I'm sure he would have helped me out and put the situation in perspective, but hey – at least he's helping us out now!

How Do You Treat Others?

Lastly, let me tell you that John is one of the kindest people I've ever met – he always treats others with respect. How you treat others is a big part of your legacy; you never know what others are going through.

I'm a warm, kind, and fun-loving guy, but I do get annoyed when other people are disrespectful for no reason. John helped me to remember that it's all about being the bigger person and treating others with kindness even if they were wrong to do what they did. I'm all for standing up for yourself, but you have to remember that what your emotions may be telling you to do at *this* moment may not be what is best for you in the long-run. Think your actions through, don't do anything impulsively, and remember that mean words can come back to bite you. There's almost never a reason to treat someone else like garbage, even if they've been mean to you.

It's up to you to strike the balance between being the bigger person and asserting yourself in a kind, but firm, way while never letting other people walk all over you. I learned from John, and this might help you as well, that sometimes the best thing you can do is to let something go and move on with your life. It's not only the mark of professionalism but also the mark of maturity and being a person who lifts others up.

Really examine how you treat others. It's the mark of your character and who you really are as a person. If you want to be a leader, then let other people save face even when you know they're wrong. Be like John and be someone who treats others with respect and kindness whenever possible. This took me years to learn, and I'm still working on it, but the truth is you never know what someone else is going through. If you can continue being kind to others, you'll make other people feel good about themselves *and* get the last laugh. What's better than that?

Serving others and encouraging other people – building them up – is a surefire way to success. When you are so focused on helping other people that you don't even have time to worry about things outside of your control, you'll know you are well on your way to reaching your Mountaintop each and every day.

Questions for Reflection

1. How can you become more involved in your community? Are there soup kitchens, homeless shelters, or other kinds of organizations where you could volunteer your time?

2. What are some ways you could shift your mentality to one of giving and service to others?

3. How can you use a focus on serving others as a way to better maintain perspective during the trials and tribulations of your life?

Chapter 10: Put Yourself Out There and Add Genuine Value to Other People's Lives

*"If you really want the key to success,
start by doing the opposite of what everyone else is doing."*
– Brad Szollose

This book is an antidote to doubt, worry, procrastination, mediocrity, and "the way things are." It contains practical questions, thoughts, and action steps to get you moving in the direction of the destiny you inherently deserve so that you make progress toward and eventually reach your Mountaintop. The content in this book, as hard as this is to believe, was never taught to me in preschool, elementary school, middle school, high school, college, or graduate school. So I feel *enormously* passionate about getting this content in other people's hands because it contains the lessons and wisdom no one ever taught to me (before I met the experts featured in this book).

Here's what I'm getting at: when I finish a speaking engagement or walk into an event, and someone wants to buy this book, I don't view that as "selling." I view it as solving a problem, filling a need, and providing a solution. In return, the currency I receive for the book is a reflection of the value I've provided.

Some people think that in order to make lots of money they have to be sleazy and cheat others. This is simply not true. Tony Robbins, now a multi-millionaire, talks about how he started out feeding the homeless on Thanksgiving Day in his book *Unlimited Power*.

"When I showed up and gave turkeys to people who otherwise had no meal, these homeless folks realized that there are people out there who care," Tony said.

I love this story because it shows that Tony built his massive success on serving others and providing value. People wonder how he's amassed so much wealth – it's largely due to the fact he is seeking new ways to add value to others.

Although in that instance he didn't get paid for it, Tony took that same mentality of serving others into other aspects of his business in life. He is now absurdly wealthy not because he is greedy, but rather because he is focused on providing massive value to others.

Always Add Value and Be Willing to Put in the Work

On that note, let's dive even deeper into this powerful notion of adding value to others because it's one of the key aspects to sustaining a Mountaintop-level life. Nick Thacker, an accomplished author we heard from earlier, also has a lot to say on this. Let's use the case study of how he has built an awesome online community to understand more deeply the power of adding value:

"To build a community online, always add value," Nick said. "Focus on helping other people and document how you're doing it. When you can, ask for a small favor and get people to sign up to your mailing list. Stay in touch and continue adding worthwhile content to their lives.

"Eventually the money and time will be there for you to spend on your projects. Then you can turn around and leverage that into a slightly larger project, and the cycle continues until the value you're providing people is so massive and unbelievable that people can't ignore you.

"This strategy is absolutely as simple as it sounds, and yes, it is extremely difficult. People want the 'easy' way out. Don't be one of them. They eventually ALL come around and realize that truly valuable things aren't bought – they're built."

Nick confirms something I've known to be true from my own research, studies, and experience. The only success secret is that there is no secret. Instead of looking for a shortcut or easy way out, figure out the best way for you to add value to other people's lives. What are your core strengths? What are you best at? Start there. Yes, there is such a thing as working smarter, but if you aren't willing to put in the hard work you're going to end up falling short of what you're capable of achieving.

"Knowing that I'm working toward something bigger than just me," Nick said, "allows me to be passionate about the lifestyle – the freedom to do a lot of different things and build stuff. I'll be passionate about the overall lifestyle far longer than I will be passionate about the individual things that make up that lifestyle."

This is why the focus needs to be on adding value to other people's lives as opposed to getting lost in your own trials and tribulations. As you zoom out, take a look at the big picture and head for your summit. Remember this: even while you are experiencing countless daily ups and downs, if you take Nick's advice, and look to be a part of something bigger than yourself, you will emerge a winner in the long-run.

"I'm human," Nick continued, "and I'm constantly reminded of my own failures and weaknesses. But I've learned, over five years of blogging and writing, that if I'm not sure what to write about, I'm probably not *doing* enough stuff – or I haven't fully grasped the significance of how something I'm working on can help someone else."

Once again, I love it. *Live* your life first and write about it second. This is a more specific way of conveying one of the overarching themes of the book: be a person of integrity, character, and leadership by being someone who teaches others how to do something after you've lived it and done it yourself. Pay it forward! Reaching your Mountaintop is all about being true to your word and practicing what you preach.

"Case in point," Nick said, "is how I've been slowly and quietly working on some really cool businesses with a partner and cowriter. It's been a huge time and energy commitment, but the end results are going to be awesome!

"The problem is that I initially thought of this stuff as separate from what my blog is about. But I was thinking about it and stressing over my empty, dead blog, and I realized that I DID have something to write about. I could write about how I'm managing my time, how I'm responding to self-doubt, how I'm motivating myself to keep working toward a goal, and how these author-service business ideas are part of my overall world-domination strategy.

"It immediately gave me about ten blog post ideas, a book idea, and a newfound interest in blogging. Marketing is not a dirty word. Marketing is simply taking something of value that you have and putting it in front of the people you KNOW would love it," Nick expressed.

"Do things that add value to other people's lives, and the long-term gains will be far greater than what you ever imagined."

Do you see what we're getting at here? You can define your life and success on your own terms as long as you keep the focus on serving and helping other people. You reach your Mountaintop by constantly serving others and adding value to their lives.

Always Be Listening

As you continue to add value and strategically move forward, remember there is enormous power in listening. I had a heart-to-heart conversation with Pat Helmers about this. Pat is the founder of Sales Babble, a website, podcast, sales training, and sales consulting resource that provides selling secrets for non-sellers. A successful salesman and entrepreneur, Pat is an inspiration.

"Adding value to others and making a difference is all about listening," Pat said. "Keep your conversations natural and continually ask good questions. That's the key to success: listening and asking good questions."

Pat shattered limitations, going from an engineering career to a sales career and choosing to fulfill his purpose. He is someone who does not limit himself in any way whatsoever. He doesn't believe in labeling himself or others. He can relate to people and is good at getting other people to talk. He claims he was never an Einstein at software, but nonetheless, becoming an engineer is a huge accomplishment. He is a man of many talents and worth listening to as we ascend the Mountaintop.

"Try this," Pat said. "Treat every person you meet like they're your cousin. Start talking to them like you know them, and they pick up on that. From experience, I can tell you they pick up on that right away. The amazing part about this is you can do this to strangers! You can ask all kinds of personal questions while being natural. You definitely don't want to be overtly creepy, but just think of them as a cousin and you'll come across as naturally yourself."

"That's awesome; I like that a lot. This strategy worked for me in my travels when I introduced myself to new people from around the world every single day. What kinds of questions would you ask your cousin?" I asked.

"*Busy day? What's your morning like?*" Pat said. "Simple stuff that establishes rapport. Shoot the breeze a little bit; have a conversation. You're not giving a speech; you're having a conversation."

"That's powerful," I said, "but it's also simple. Why don't more people follow this process?"

"Great question," Pat said. "It may be simple, but you'd be surprised how many people jump right into talking about themselves. It's not about that. Those kinds of people have the process backward. It's alright to talk about yourself, but first, learn about the person you are talking with. In return, they'll naturally want to know about you. What are their problems and struggles? How can you add value to their lives without expecting anything in return? It's about being friendly, identifying needs, and presenting win-win solutions. If you're not interested in helping others, then don't create a business."

Pat mirrors Chris Salem's wisdom from earlier in this book: the irony here is that when you are detached from the outcome of a given conversation, that's when genuine business opportunities will come from your interactions with others. The purpose here is to reach your Mountaintop, not necessarily to create a business, but creating a business can certainly be part of it. Whatever you choose as your focus, have the character to truly care about others by getting to know them and asking relevant questions. That's what putting yourself out there and adding value to other people's lives is about.

Make the Human Connection

Trevor Smith is President and CEO of Blue Sky Consulting, and I met him at a networking group in the Northeast. As a consultant, trainer, and professional speaker, Trevor impacts, inspires, and helps organizations by teaching teamwork and communication skills while showing how to bring more humor and lightness to everyday work life. Trevor speaks to everyone, from non-profit organizations and healthcare corporations to colleges and universities. He makes a solid impact – his insights tie perfectly into this chapter in terms of really putting yourself out there and adding value to other people's lives.

"Want a simple yet incredibly powerful secret?" Trevor asked me. "Meet with people in person as often as you reasonably can. Offer to help others. There are so many people in the world who don't care about others, so when you offer to genuinely help and listen to others, you are in the elite few."

I nodded, realizing that we were getting right down to brass tacks in the quaint *Prime 16* restaurant we were sitting in while having this discussion.

"Linkedin, Twitter, Facebook, that stuff is all great when used properly," Trevor continued. "But the key is those tools must be used as a *complement* to in-person meetings, not as a substitute. The problem is that people forget to make the human connection. When you go out of your way to really meet people and get to know them, you will automatically be setting yourself up to succeed."

These are powerful insights, and I agree with Trevor completely.

"Don't let the few bad eggs take away from the many good eggs," Trevor said. "Because there are way more good eggs than there are bad eggs. You get business from word of mouth and networking. I encourage you to help others, and I also encourage you to let others know how they can help you. People will help you if only you show them how. Think of it as developing win-win relationships."

Nodding my head, and soaking in his wisdom, while blocking out the chatter around me on that Wednesday evening in a New Haven, Connecticut, restaurant, I got a good vibe from Trevor.

"There are a lot of opportunities out there," Trevor said. "Always look for opportunities and how you can take advantage of ways to add value to other people's lives. Don't ever limit yourself. And don't let small discouragements get in the way of the possibility of big victories."

Trevor is authentic – someone who genuinely wants to get you to your Mountaintop (just like everyone else I've interviewed for this book). I'm lucky and grateful to have spoken with him. Winners like Trevor are always looking for ways to lift other people up and encourage them.

The way Trevor discovered his current business opportunity is fascinating, to say the least. He worked in the human resources field for twenty years and used his job as an incubator for business opportunities. Specifically, he was proactive on the job and asked his manager if he could be one of the trainers for group sessions. This started out as a once-a-month thing but grew from there. I share this with you because Trevor's life acts as a great case study for adding value to the world and reaching your Mountaintop.

Taking the bull by the horns, Trevor went through a certified program in which he built expertise in bringing laughter to the workplace through group work and programs.

My advice to you, supported by the people I've featured in this book, is if your current job isn't working, find another job to incubate your dream. Don't be afraid to leave a job that isn't right for you. Despite what the naysayers were saying to me beforehand, when I finally left a job that was wrong for me it was the greatest feeling in the world. I said this earlier, and I'm emphasizing it again because it's incredibly easy to feel trapped in your current situation, like there's no way out. Remind yourself that there are possibilities and solutions.

If you have a family to feed, then I completely understand not being able to just walk out, but the point is to refuse to settle. Continue to take action and look for that right opportunity. Don't feel like you have to go straight from where you are to a business owner (if being a business owner is your goal); as Trevor's life story clearly indicates, a powerful and practical way is to go step-by-step by using your job as a springboard – a springboard to your Mountaintop. And it's completely alright to go from one job to another while growing your dream if that's what you feel is your best move.

And like we heard from Brian Olds and other experts in this book, reaching your Mountaintop is not so much about rushing to the end goal as it is steadily making progress each and every day. Have a vision and then take action on that vision one day at a time.

While in the human services field, Trevor noticed a lack of training for:

- Communication
- Teamwork/teambuilding
- Collaboration
- Daily conflict and problem-solving

It would be easy to look past those skills as commonplace and ordinary, but Trevor thought differently. He didn't limit himself, and he became a careful observer of everything. He used his job as an opportunity to figure out what the biggest problems and challenges in the workplace were. *He found a way to add value by identifying a problem and then solving it.*

Rather than thinking of your job as punishment, think of it as a training ground and learning opportunity. Even if you're not in love with your job, there are small opportunities and pockets in each day to focus on the aspects which you love.

"I saw there was a real need to help organizations keep more employees while creating a positive work culture," Trevor said. "I realized there was nothing else out there like I was doing."

Trevor's focus on creating humor in the workplace, while teaching valuable and practical skills, is what makes him such a sought-after consultant. After all, today's turnover rates are at an all-time high.

"We all get hit with roadblocks," Trevor said, "but even when dealing with them, do what you love to do. Follow your passion. The way to get past your ups and downs is to really believe in what you're doing. Keep networking and getting out there. I know as much as anyone else that business can be slow at times, but if you keep on pushing forward past the roadblocks you will find the success you're looking for."

"So success is not really about get-rich-quick schemes or quick-fixes," I said. "It's more about finding the ability to push forward and get comfortable with the everyday routine. It's about embracing the grind."

"That's right," Trevor said. "We all face monotony. We all face things we don't want to do. But the winners are the ones who push past that and continue anyway. Those are the ones who end up winning and succeeding."

"It's almost like people see the end result," I said. "But they don't realize all the hard work that went into it. There are a lot of steps and factors that go into reaching your Mountaintop, and it doesn't happen all at once."

"Exactly," Trevor said. "People don't see successful people grinding away late at night on a weekend; they see the success and have no idea what it took to get there. I stand out amongst my competition because I fully, truly, 100% believe in what I'm doing, and clients pick up on that. They pick up on my energy, and when they see all the preparation I'm willing to do before the speaking engagement actually occurs, they realize that I'm the real deal."

Trevor speaks professionally for a living. It's clear that Trevor leads by example because he practices what he preaches and lives what he learns. It's not about trying to get money from people. It's about making sure you *give* value.

The Way to Add Value Is to Be True to Yourself

Entrepreneur and life coach Michelle Demers is an expert we heard from in chapter seven, the time management chapter. Her inspiring story shows how you can transition into what you were meant to do so that you can best add value to other people and the world. She told me about a study abroad program she did in Mexico when she was in school. This program was about marine biology and she absolutely loved taking boats out, using off-weeks to travel, staying at local hotels in close quarters with six other people (including sleeping in the middle of the desert), and staying in primitive areas. It gave her a strong grasp of what goes on in our world and opened her mind to new possibilities.

This resonated with me. My study abroad adventure in Budapest, Hungary, my entire junior year of college – when I lived, worked, studied, and played baseball in Europe for a full calendar year – was the turning point in my life. When I say it opened my eyes to the world, I don't mean that in some grandiose, impractical way. I mean it legitimately allowed me the opportunity to travel to dozens of countries across Europe and Asia, meet hundreds of new people, and be exposed to realities and situations I never before thought possible (both good and bad). My year in Europe was the first time in my life when the pieces of the puzzle of my life came together, and I was enjoying and appreciating life each day. I was finally able to put things in perspective by realizing that the key to being successful is to add value to other people.

How this applies to you is that you will have many situations in your life which will turn out unexpectedly or in a bad way. The tendency for us all is to become negative and angry about the setbacks. But what Michelle is telling you, and my life experience confirms, is that if you keep pushing forward the puzzle pieces will come together, often in surprising ways. Once the puzzle pieces come together, you will understand how you can best take action and help other people.

"Life is a really windy path," Michelle said. "For a while, I was totally anti-business, into animals and the non-profit scene. My view on business was that it was greedy, involving snake-oil salesmen, boring jobs, and imprisoning cubicles.

"But then I read the book, *Ben and Jerry's*, and discovered how the founders of Ben and Jerry's created their business in the same town that my college, University of Vermont, is located. Their business was all about social good, giving back to the community through charities and other initiatives by genuinely adding value to the world. It caused me to realize, *gosh, business isn't all that bad, and if you're in business you can make a lot of money and do good things with that.*"

"I read that book as well," I said. "It's one of the books my dad suggested I read while I was in college and it's incredibly powerful the way Ben and Jerry founded their business on strong social principles."

"Yes," Michelle said. "After reading that book and doing a little reflecting, I made a 180-degree turn in my life. I *transitioned* by getting in the driver's seat of my life. I went and got my MBA from Rutgers. I was still struggling with the idea of working in a corporate environment; cubicles just didn't feel right to me. But, I undoubtedly was now interested in business. It doesn't matter what the turning point in your life is as you long as you make the turn. For me, it was reading a valuable book."

I'm going to repeat that because it's so powerful: **It doesn't matter what the turning point in your life is as you long as you make the turn.** If your turning point is something epic or climactic, that's awesome. But your turning point can also be entering into a good conversation, reading an enlightening book, or taking a moment of silent reflection for yourself.

Notice how Michelle said that cubicles just didn't feel right to her. The key here is to do what feels right to you. Michelle is not telling you to avoid cubicle jobs specifically. I have worked cubicle jobs that were fantastic and caused me to grow, have fun, and meet great people. If you enjoy where you're at now, then that's amazing, and you are successful in your own right. Michelle is suggesting to do what feels right to you and then find a way to fill that vocation with a job, passion, business, or hobby that brings meaning and purpose to you while adding value to others.

"What resonated with me and really got me moving forward in my transition is when I learned about coaching: how to integrate life coaching with business coaching," Michelle said. "I got started in the coaching profession and have been there ever since. I've gotten away from my original passion for wildlife and environment, but I'm hoping to be philanthropic, so I have time to volunteer and be physically active. I'm using my business as a way to come back around full circle to my career dreams of marine biology, helping all wildlife, gravitating towards marine causes, turtles in Costa Rica, stuff like that. In the meantime, I continue to add value to other people through my coaching programs and services."

Michelle's multiple passions are fascinating, and she's making an impact. Notice also, she is not using business as a means to an end; she is enjoying the journey along the way. Just because you aren't able to monetize one of your passions right away doesn't mean you won't be actively involved in it or end up making money from it at some point in the future. It means life wants to take you down other roads first to learn valuable lessons and make an impact in other areas. Everything that happens is meant to be, and as you can see, there are ways to create win-win scenarios in life where one passion leads into the next.

"I love the lifestyle of doing what I love while making money. I've built my business around the idea and daily practice of helping others," Michelle said. "That's what business is all about. I've come full circle, and now I love business. I'm creating all sorts of new businesses, and I'm implementing strategies that are helping me to grow wealth by adding value to others."

Money is a means to help other people. Lots of money is a good thing, not a bad thing, and can be used appropriately when in the right hands. Money will amplify who you are, so if you have strong character, values, and morals, you will manage your wealth responsibly. Also, note how Michelle talked about life coming full circle. A transition is really about returning to your roots and doing what you're best at. It's a return to the reason why you are here on the planet, connecting with your specific mission and purpose. It's also a return to adding value and being of service to others.

Live a Life of Meaning, Purpose, Value, and Service

The stories in this chapter are amazing examples of breaking free of the mold, staying true to yourself, and living a life of meaning, purpose, value, and service. That's Mountaintop-living at its finest. As we head into the final chapter of this book and put it all together, prepare to embrace the incredible power of your mind.

Questions for Reflection

1. What are some ways you could add value to your family, friends, job, vocation, business, and/or other endeavors? What are some of the problems you could solve?

2. Is it time to reinvent yourself? Is it time to transition to another job or career? Is it time to put more focus on something you truly care about, so you are better positioned to uniquely add value to the world?

3. What are some of the metrics in your version of success? What are the aspects of success for you other than money? What does your ideal day look like in terms of putting yourself out there and helping others? What are some local, national, or international events you could attend to meet more people?

Chapter 11: Visualize Your Way to the Mountaintop

"The Mountaintop is usually not a destination or place. It's the feeling you get when you stay focused, avoid distractions, and push past roadblocks. It's a way of thinking, acting, and being. It's being more concerned with making an impact and helping those in need than needlessly worrying about the opinions of others."
– Jeff Davis

My conversation with relationship expert and radio show host Harvey Bailey happened in divine order. I met him through Parkville Toastmasters (while I was living and working in Maryland) and our relationship transcended the club – we ended up becoming close friends. Although I no longer live in the Maryland area, we stayed in touch, and this conversation happened on a return trip to Maryland.

Harvey is an author and professional speaker. He's also an ordained Reverend, a certified Reiki instructor, and a master of mental science. He gives off the best vibe in the world, and it's a pleasure to be in his calm, assured presence. He exudes love not as an idea or concept, but as a way of being. Love is more than an emotion: it's a power that connects us all.

Harvey will show you that you are destined for greatness. He's the perfect end to this book, the cherry on top of the whipped cream, the ace in the hole. When you take what we've already discussed and mix in the following mental science laws, you have the recipe for success and making a real impact in the world. Let's head for the Mountaintop and leave the haters in the dust!

Serendipity

The journey of life is no cakewalk, and Harvey knows that better than anyone. Having already overcome setbacks earlier in his life, he knows how to handle the curveballs and twists and turns in life. (Type into YouTube, "Survival Harvey Bailey," to see his epic speech which I filmed for him as he was speaking at one of Brian Olds's SKILLS events in September of 2013. The YouTube link is titled with one word: *Survival*.)

It turns out the weekend I went to see Harvey in person to feature him in this book was quite serendipitous, because Harvey had *just* broken through to a new level of success by landing some great client deals, speaking engagements, coaching sessions, and seminars of all sorts. Harvey overcame the early stages of the entrepreneur's journey and took his business, and life, to a whole new level. To Harvey, the key to reaching your Mountaintop is trusting in God.

"I promised myself that I would let go and trust in God more," Harvey said. "And that's easy to do when everything is going well, but when the bills run high, and the income runs low, the doubts start coming on and it becomes a lot harder to maintain that trust. I'm growing my business and running my seminars to help people flourish in their lives and relationships, and my business partner and I are a good match. But it's not always easy to get everyone we want to our seminars and sometimes the people who sign up don't show up.

"In the past, I might have let that get me down," Harvey continued. "But, now that I've increased my trust in God that everything will work out, I just keep on going and pushing forward. When I finally saw deals come in that were able to sustain me, it was a mixture of action and serendipity. Sometimes I would get calls out of the blue from people who turned into perfect coaching clients, and sometimes I would have to work like crazy to create the right opportunities for my business. But, throughout it all, I knew God would always provide for me the right opportunities at the right time.

"I went through some struggles and could have quit my business, but I knew this was an opportunity to deepen my trust in God," Harvey expressed. "I knew this was what I wanted to do – be a speaker, coach, relationship expert, seminar leader, and entrepreneur – and I wasn't about to let that go. Although some people around me were doubting, I kept putting myself out there. Eventually, right in the nick of time, I landed the business I needed to push me forward. It came from a trust in both myself and God.

"It was not as hard as I thought it would be. Yes, obviously, I went through some struggles, and it wasn't always easy, but looking back on it I now know that taking action is a lot more powerful than we may initially think. Even with my back up against the wall, a relatively small amount of purposeful action went a long way."

Harvey's story is inspirational, to say the least. He made it happen by forging his own luck and deepening his spiritual connection to a higher power, something that would benefit us all. What I learned from Harvey's story and adventure is that most of our obstacles come from within.

It's not that our goals and dreams are impossible and the world is plotting against us – rather, it's exactly the opposite. Our goals and dreams are closer than we realize and when we take action – that first step –

previously unseen forces emerge from the ether to assist us in moving forward.

When was the last time you spent a whole day thinking about nothing but your goal? When was the last time you took massive action, without being overly concerned about rejection and external circumstances, even when your back was up against the wall? Let's both learn from Harvey's example and remind ourselves to take more action each and every day. Action is the key to success.

Creativity, Breathing, and Visualization

"This is great stuff my friend," I said. "And you certainly are a wise man. Another thought comes to mind: a big challenge for a lot of us is that we have more than one passion. How do we know which one to focus on?"

"Become creative and combine two loves," Harvey said. "For example, there are plenty of people who have found ways to merge travel with their profession, if travel is one of their loves. Think of a win-win solution, some kind of permutation that may not have been initially obvious. Look for people who have done what you want to do and then figure out how to use their model but in your own unique way.

"Creating a vision board changed my life and it can change yours as well. It took things to the next level. In that vision board, write out exactly how you want it to work. Do you want your boyfriend/girlfriend to stay with you and travel with you? Put it on the vision board. Then send energies into the vision board and let that reality manifest. For example, if you want to move overseas start looking at places overseas; start considering options, but don't be locked in as to how it's going to happen. Then leave it to the universe as to how it will be created.

"Do some visualization; sit there and see it in your mind," added Harvey. "Don't be attached to HOW it's supposed to happen, just see it happening – see yourself overseas, see your girl there with you, and let the universe fill in the blanks."

"I like all of this," I said. "In fact, I love all of it, and I will be putting it into practice, as will others. A big question that comes up though is what about people who struggle with visualization, who say it's not for them?"

"For people who have trouble with visualization, the answer is usually just in clearing their mind. When they concentrate on their breathing for a number of days and weeks, it allows their awareness to grow. They can push those negative thoughts out of their minds by thinking, or saying out loud, *cancel, cancel,* or, *zero, zero,*" Harvey answered.

"My suggestion is to create a schedule where for the first three weeks," Harvey further explained, "you do nothing but focus on your breathing and observing your breath. In week four, don't focus on the breath, but rather focus on clearing the mind. During weeks five through eight, combine the breathing with the clear mind, and then weeks nine through twelve are all about visualization."

You may, of course, customize this process to suit your schedule and needs. You may even want to go straight to the visualization. With that said, this is the process that has worked incredibly well for Harvey to reach his Mountaintop, as well as for many others that he has spoken with and coached. In short, this is a process that has led to practical results for people just like you and me.

If you are ridiculously busy, start with a few minutes of breathing and visualization time each day.

"The first three weeks of this process is just observing your breath for fifteen minutes a day," Harvey added. "By the end of the fourth week, work up to thirty minutes. And remember, week four is about clearing the mind.

"Most people don't breathe properly," Harvey explained. "When you breathe in, breathe deep into the diaphragm and create a Buddha belly pointing out. This is what will take you to the alpha state. On the exhale, push the belly in."

I tend to do the opposite of what Harvey suggested with my breathing, based on the way I push my belly in on the inhale and out on the exhale. I trust Harvey with this process because I know he's an expert, so I'm going to do what he is suggesting here.

Do what works for you, but try out Harvey's suggestions and see if they add quality to your life. They certainly have worked wonders for me.

Mind Control

"Thoughts are like anything else," Harvey said. "You may remove them at will. That's where mind control methods come into play when reaching and sustaining your own version of success. I'm a big fan of the Silva Mind Control methods, as I've taken several Silva Method courses and a lot of the advice I give on meditation came from what I learned there.

"As far as the Silva teachings, at a basic level, it's all about clearing your mind with deep breathing. Count down from 3 to 1, going down to the alpha mindset. Then put the vision, the final result, of what you want to achieve in your mind. Do this every day until you achieve the particular goal or result you want.

"It's always a learning process," Harvey added. "So be patient and loving with yourself and try to make light of the frustrations. Even the so-called gurus and experts haven't mastered this process, so remember it's just about practicing, making time, and moving forward."

Parting Words

"Stay focused," Harvey said. "Go within to learn about yourself because not enough people know themselves well, if at all. Never stop learning, never stop growing, and never stop trying. And most importantly, stay connected to God.

"When you are going after your goals, dreams, career aspirations, and business plans, break it down into the steps you need to move forward. Continually ask yourself what skills you need to learn, what you need to study, who you need to get to know (investors, potential sponsors, etc.), and what you need to master to get to where you want to be.

"Another tip I recommend is doing a cost analysis of your business idea. Make sure it's at least a somewhat viable idea, even if you have to look out into the future to plan for your own success. This is what will allow you to budget, buy business cards, set up a website, and do that *one thing* that is needed to move you forward.

"Measure where you are moving toward; if it's achievable, someone else has probably done it. Just make sure it's realistic. And when I say realistic, I am talking about it being realistic to YOU, not to others. Also, create a time frame, which is a specific date when certain stages of the process will be successfully launched. **Your success**

doesn't depend on what other people think, so don't worry about that either. Don't be afraid to strike off on your own and do your own thing.

"Also, don't be vague. Let your mind go to work with specific timeframes and action lists. Then, every day, you can do at least one thing on your to-do list to move in the direction of the success you want to create. And you can add momentum to that by taking it into prayer and visualization. Like all things in life you get out what you put in, so the more energy you put into it, the more you will get out of it."

I'm sure, by now, you can tell why I'm so impressed with this man. He worked for his success while applying the Mountaintop way of life to *speed up the process* of his success significantly. You will never once, ever, hear me say there is a shortcut to success. But you will hear me say, time and time again, both through my own words and the words of the experts I have interviewed, that there is a way to be successful, happy, liberated, and free *without* compromising your happiness. In addition, you can successfully maintain your peace of mind and sanity, with reduced stress.

The path of least resistance doesn't include any shortcuts. Rather, the path of least resistance is the most effective way to your Mountaintop. It's the path that cuts out the naysayers and allows you to focus in on what YOU want so that you may effectively help others in your unique way.

Visualization worked incredibly well for me when I competed in the 2014 District 53 Toastmasters International Speech Competition. Competing against some of the best speakers in the Northeast, I had my work cut out for me. Not many people thought I could win, but I continued to visualize the desired outcome of holding the first-place trophy. I imagined the feeling of connecting with the audience and sharing an epic message. Before the big day, I held the feeling in my heart, mind, and soul of making a difference and achieving victory.

My speech was called *Someday is Today*. My message was, time is incredibly short, and our lives can be taken from us unexpectedly at any time. My three tips to the audience to live their dreams were as follows. One, be disciplined on a daily basis by making time to work on your goal. Two, collaborate with others and figure out ways to get around the right people. And three, push past rejection. Every no is one step closer to a yes.

I was speaker seven of seven in the contest, and I gave the speech of my life. I won first place and was crowned as one of the best speakers in the world. My authenticity came through, and I made a genuine connection with the audience exactly as I imagined and visualized it happening. I say this for no reason other than to show you what's possible. Winning this contest completely changed my life in every way, opening doors of opportunity and possibility, and jumpstarting my professional speaking career. There are no limits. I believe in you.

In the end, it's about what success means to you, not someone else. Use the power of your mind to give you the edge as you go after what you want. Apply the steps in this book and watch as your life improves for the better. You will have setbacks and down days, but on the whole, you will make progress and get from where you are to where you want to be. It's been an absolute honor to have you on this journey with me, and I'm eternally grateful you've considered these words. Blow by the haters, critics, and naysayers by staying true to yourself. This is your life to live and no one else's. You've got this. See you at the Mountaintop.

Questions for Reflection

1. What do you want to put on your vision board? What are some ways you can keep your goals, dreams, and vision in front of you on a regular basis?

2. What is your biggest and most audacious goal? What end result would make sense for you to start visualizing in your free time?

3. What one project or task would, upon completion, fill you with the greatest sense of meaning, purpose, and power?

Epilogue

"It's not lonely at the top if you help someone else get there."
– Aaron Darko

You got to know me a little bit in the first chapter when I talked about that unexpected setback I had while in high school. I was excited to go to college, but I psychologically limped into college life with a lot of insecurities because my senior year of high school turned out so poorly.

McDaniel College was the perfect stepping stone at the time I needed it most. I grew and evolved, met awesome people, and once again opened up to the possibilities life has to offer. It definitely didn't happen all at once and my freshman and sophomore year of college had shaky days, weeks, and even months as I slowly grew out of my doubtful ways. But, regardless of the roadblocks, the general trend of my life was onwards and upwards. Senior year of college was awesome, and I landed a good job in a difficult economy.

In October of 2015, I returned to McDaniel College for Homecoming. It was my first homecoming in about three years, after doing lots of speaking around the world and publishing my first book. On Saturday morning I went to a wonderful dedication ceremony of the new fountain on campus and then afterward I went to the GOLD (Graduates of the Last Decade) brunch. It was there I bumped into Warren, one of my friends from college. Warren is a leader, firmly grounded in his values and a source of kindness to all who know him.

I had some good friends from college, but because I spontaneously decided to go to this Homecoming I didn't have any set plans (this is my way of traveling), so bumping into Warren was perfect. We also recently reconnected on Facebook, so it was good timing.

"You've done a lot," Warren said, "and have really come a long way since college."

We talked about our lives since college and what we've been up to. I filled Warren in on some of my travels around the world as well as various keynote speaking engagements. Warren does an incredible job of showing genuine interest in others, a key quality of becoming successful.

After catching up at the brunch, we continued chatting on our way to the football field where the big game was happening. During the game we parted ways for a bit, to see our respective friends. I saw some of my friends from college and also hung out with a really great group of people from Philadelphia I met the night before, alumni who graduated about seven years before I did.

At the end of homecoming, while I was sitting down in a serene moment of reflection while people were clearing out, Warren came up to me again and saw the glimmer in my eye.

This was a magical moment because I'd come so far – I say this as genuinely and sincerely as possible – and after years of so many temporary setbacks, defeats, anxieties, and failures, I'd made a comeback and was now at peace.

"We're already at the Mountaintop," Warren said, "and don't even realize it. We're already there."

Warren knows about the idea of reaching your Mountaintop because he has been following my adventures on Facebook and Instagram, where I often talk about this powerful concept.

"Yes," I said, "yes, my friend. Very well said. We are already there."

We looked up to the sun – the beautiful sun searing into a late afternoon, mid-October sky – and we both smiled.

"Life comes full circle," I said to Warren, "and even the most unfair and unexpected of circumstances have a way of working themselves out."

See you at The Mountaintop.

Questions for Reflection

1. How can you create a happy ending for yourself? What is the ideal outcome of the challenge, setback, difficult, and/or unwanted event you are experiencing? What is the silver lining?

2. Who are some people you could surround yourself with that make you feel like a million bucks and like anything is possible?

3. What do you want to be said about you in your epitaph at your funeral? What do you want to be written on your tombstone? How do you want to be remembered? What legacy do you want to leave? How can you begin leaving this legacy starting today?

Book Jeff to Speak and Additional Information

Speaker Jeff Davis is an internationally-renowned professional keynote speaker. He speaks to students, nonprofits, businesses, conferences, associations, and all sorts of organizations. His expertise is in helping people, especially high school and college students, get through dark and challenging times. He shares practical strategies on how to deal with adversity. His keynote speaking topics include suicide prevention, anti-bullying, dealing with pressure & stress, improving work/life balance, mastering time management, and becoming a better leader. His Twitter handle is jeffdavis027, and his Instagram handle is jld016. You can also find him on Facebook via Facebook.com/authorjeffdavis, on Pinterest via @authorjeffdavis, on LinkedIn via LinkedIn.com/speakerjeffdavis, and on Google+ as +JeffreyDavisMountaintop27. To subscribe to his YouTube channel, type "Speaker Jeff Davis" into the YouTube search bar or go to Youtube.com/user/27JeffDavis.

If you know someone who would benefit from this book, please refer them to this content. If you know of an audience who would benefit from Jeff's message, please let Jeff's team know.

To book Jeff as a keynote speaker for your next event, please visit jeffdspeaks.com or contact Jeff's Executive Assistant Meg at meg@jeffdspeaks.com.

If you would like to reach out to Jeff directly via a question, comment, or general thought, his email is jeff@jeffdspeaks.com or davisjeffrey222@gmail.com.

Experts Featured in This Book

The people listed below are people I *featured* in this book (the list does not include other authors and luminaries I quoted at chapter beginnings, whom I did not feature at greater length). If no email is listed beneath the expert's name, please go to their website for more information on how to get in touch with them. If an expert is featured in more than one chapter, as several of them are, they are grouped into the chapter in which they appear first. If you have any additional questions for these awesome and revolutionary thought leaders, please reach out to them.

Chapter 1

Dan Blanchard
granddaddyssecrets.com

Chapter 2

Dr. Dorothy Martin-Neville
askdrdorothy.com

Daniel Midson-Short
midsonshort.com

Ravi Wettasinghe
He can be found on LinkedIn

Dananjaya Hettiarachchi
iseesomethinginyou.com
facebook.com/dananjayajhettiarachchi
He can also be found on LinkedIn

Nick Thacker
writehacked.com

Geeta Nadkarni
geetanadkarni.com

Randy Gage
randygage.com

Chapter 3

Jenn Scalia
jennscalia.com

Chris Salem
christophersalem.com
chris@christophersalem.com

Jenny Drescher
bridgetochoice.com
jenny@bridgetochoice.com
connectandimprov@gmail.com

Chapter 4

Heather Hansen O'Neill
fireinfive.com

Bill Corbett
billcorbett.com

Ann Meacham
She can be found on LinkedIn

Mike Shelah
mikeshelah.com
He can also be found on LinkedIn

Chapter 5

Michael Benner
michaelbenner.com
mb@michaelbenner.com

Christine Southworth
southworthwellness@gmail.com

Chapter 6

Dave Wheeler
gps-speakermarketing.com
dmarkwheeler.com
thewishbuilder.com
dave@dmarkwheeler.com

Michael Lynch
michaeljlynch.com
michael@michaeljlynch.com

Chapter 7

John Lee Dumas
eofire.com

Rick Woods
tforganizer.com
tforganizer@att.net

Chip Janiszewski
chipj.com
happinessandsuccessgps.com
chip@chipj.com

Michelle Demers
joingroupology.com
md.groupology@gmail.com

Chapter 8

Brian Olds
yournewskills.com
brianjolds@yournewskills.com

Chapter 9

John Powers
johnjosephpowers.com
john@drmissionteam.org

Chapter 10

Pat Helmers
salesbabble.com
pathelmers@salesbabble.com

Trevor Smith
blueskyconsulting.us
tsmith@blueskyconsulting.us

Chapter 11

Harvey Bailey
oneloveoneconnectiononeus.com
theonethought@gmail.com

About **Jeff Davis**...

Jeff Davis, a.k.a. Mr. Mountaintop, is an author, blogger, professional speaker, marketer, world traveler, consultant, and humanitarian. He has done keynote speeches internationally and is a sought-after expert on suicide prevention and overcoming adversity. Jeff did a TEDx talk in New York City called *How to Fulfill Your Inner Life,* and he frequently speaks to high schools, colleges, nonprofits, organizations, associations, conferences, and businesses. He is a resident of the world. To get in touch with Jeff, please email him at jeff@jeffdspeaks.com or connect with him on Twitter via @JeffDavis027.

CPSIA information can be obtained
at www.ICGtesting.com
Printed in the USA
BVOW11s0858160317
478572BV00003B/265/P